CC   .ɔ

A MIDWIFE IN AFRICA

By Mona McAlpine

Dedicated to my granddaughter, Catriona Eilidh McAlpine

CHAPTER ONE

A two-year plan

July 1969

Morning, Mrs McAlpine. This is James, from Samorgan Glasgow. Is your husband at home?'

Husband! I give myself a shake. Of course, I'm married, albeit only for a month.

'He's at work, I'm afraid. Can I take a message?' Samorgan is the agency that's arranging our emigration to South Africa.

'Well, Mrs McAlpine, I have good news for you. You'll be off mid-October.'

I barely hear the rest of the conversation; my mind being focused on how soon we'll be leaving behind everything I've ever known.

Phew! Truth is, now that our plans and schemes are becoming reality, I'm not sure what to think. I'm glad Iain will only be home later today. At least I'll have some time by myself, time to think about my final decision.

It's a cold mid-summer day in 1969, but you wouldn't know it by the sound of the lashing rain on our window. I look out on a dreich Shetland landscape of soft hills and heather, and try to imagine what South Africa might look like.

It conjures all kinds of images in my fertile brain, but sunny is surely the principal word. Sunny South Africa. That sounds good to me. One of the best climates in the world – that sounds even better. Safaris, lions and cheetahs, gold mines, diamond mines, Table Mountain ... I'm excited at the very thought. I open our front door and take a walk through the tiny garden, where the north-east wind nearly blows me over. 'Nah,' I exclaim out loud, 'there's no competition.'

Just a few months ago, I had never heard the name Samorgan. As for South Africa, apart from the enticing brochures supplied by the company, which have filled my head with images of elephants, gold mines and a perfect climate, all I really know about the country is what I learnt at school. I have a vague memory of the Boer War but, truth to tell, I can't even remember who won.

A year ago, Iain and I got engaged. Two years ago, I returned home to Shetland from Edinburgh to take up my new post in Lerwick as a triple duty nurse – district nurse, midwife and health visitor. And no sooner back I met my husband to be. My Iain, the man I'd been waiting for all my life, and up he popped right under my nose.

Fate does have a way of intervening in our lives. Iain had just been accepted by a construction company who won a tender for a big project in South Africa. And then I came along. Once our relationship became serious and marriage was on the cards, he was all for withdrawing from his contract, he could see how happy I was to be home in Shetland. When he voiced his decision, though, I promptly replied: 'When are we going? I'm all set for a new adventure.'

'Be serious, Mona, think about it. We'll have to stay

there for two years. What if you hate the place? What if you're homesick?' The 'what ifs' went on and on. We discussed every subject in detail, from the absence of family support to the apartheid government.

Iain has a far better handle on what to expect than I have. He has made it his business to learn as much as possible about South Africa. The stack of books and reading material in our house is evidence of that. Obviously, he has given this a lot of thought.

Unlike Iain, I'm a spontaneous, live-for-today, let-tomorrow-take-care-of-itself kind of girl. I love adventure and, as for homesickness, I am long over that malady, having lived and worked in five major British cities since the age of fifteen. The City of Gold, Johannesburg, sounds exciting. Surely it can't be so very different from what I'm used to? I've decided that I will meet all the 'what ifs' when and if they arise. Now I have someone by my side who is also up for a challenge, I have only to persuade Iain to follow his dream. By the time he arrives home, dinner is ready. I have made a special effort: a roast leg of Shetland lamb, new tatties and home-grown vegetables. I even have a bottle of wine cooling in the fridge.

'What's with the celebration?' Iain is looking decidedly curious.

A long conversation ensues and, yet again, we go over the pros and cons of living in South Africa. It ends with me giving my dear husband a reassuring hug and telling him I know he will take care of me, whatever happens. I am rewarded with a hearty laugh and an excited, 'Okay, let's do it. I'll phone James in the morning.'

We lift our glasses and give a toast to South Africa, then settle down and watch the preparations for the moon landing.

Four months after our marriage, on 11 June 1969, we set off for South Africa.

On 20 July 1969, Commander Neil Armstrong stepped onto the surface of the moon.

On 15 October 1969, my twenty seventh birthday, Iain and I stepped off the plane onto the hot and dusty tarmac of Jan Smuts Airport in Johannesburg, South Africa.

CHAPTER TWO

New beginnings and cockroaches

October 1969

The first thing to tickle my senses is the smell. I turn to Iain, who has a good grip on my hand. 'Can you smell it?'

'Oh, you and your imagination,' Despite being sleep-deprived and decidedly uncomfortable after twelve hours in the air, Iain is laughing. 'Yes, you're right, I can smell it.'

We both sniff deeply, enjoying the earthy aroma. The smell of Africa.

'The sky, Iain, just look at that sky,' I'm like an excited child. There seems to be miles and miles of clear sky above us, without even the whisper of a fluffy cloud, making us both stop and stare. It's a breath-taking first impression of Mother Africa for two Scottish souls who have never seen quite so much blue.

The sun is hot on our faces. It's a short walk across the hot tarmac to the airport arrivals counter, staffed by men in khaki uniforms who speak a strange language. We've never heard it spoken before, but reckon this must be Afrikaans, which we already know to be one of the country's two official languages. The man who attends to our immigration papers and passports is not friendly. Brusque and dismissive is my impression.

'He might well be thinking about the Boer War,' Iain whispers in my ear. 'Pay no attention and give him one of your bright smiles.' I try, but it doesn't impress him.

Having given us the beady once over, Mr Unfriendly mutters something in Afrikaans. He appears unwilling to allow the English words to cross his tongue. When we don't move, he gives a tight wave, from which we gather that we're free to go. Iain says a curt thank you, before retrieving our luggage and making for the exit, with me at his side.

Surprise, surprise, the last thing we expect to see in the arrivals hall is two Shetlanders, waving and greeting us with loud hello's. We are delighted. Ian and Patsy Mundie are both well-known to my Iain. He went to school with Ian and, as part of my district nursing duties in Lerwick, I attended Ian's father. It was he who told his son that we were on our way to Johannesburg. They kept this a secret, though, in order to surprise us.

It is good to see Ian and Patsy and, on the way to their spacious apartment, they fill us in on life in Johannesburg. We are tired and find it difficult to take too much in, but we spend a homely day with them and their two school-going children, before they drive us to the Pelican, the immigrant hotel, in Kerk Street, central Johannesburg.

***

To say that the Pelican Hotel is a disappointment is an understatement. As we enter the dark room, whose floor creaks alarmingly beneath our feet, my nose immediately tells me that something's up. I can't work out why there is a strong smell of paraffin about the place, so, first chance I get, I corner the woman who cleans our room. 'That's to kill the cockroaches,' she says.

The minute we set foot in the decrepit old place, we

decide to get out as soon as possible but, for the moment, we have to grin and bear it. One immigrant family who came over on the same plane take one look, immediately turn tail and retreat to the airport, en route to Scotland. They have two little children so we can't blame them.

During our first week, we begin our hunt for a flat and, as luck would have it, we find a tidy furnished bachelor flat on the tenth floor of High Hilton, a sixteen-floor block in the cosmopolitan suburb of Hillbrow. Good show, we'll be moving in next week.

We're determined not to waste the time we have before Iain starts work. We make plans to walk the streets of Jo'burg, orienting ourselves and experiencing the sights and sounds of the city.

The Pelican might be a non-starter, but we find ourselves entranced by Johannesburg's history. We scour libraries and museums to find out more. We pester the South Africans whom we meet in the hotel for first-hand stories about their home city. Most are accommodating and pleased by our interest, and we learn fast. We discover that gold was discovered on a Transvaal farm, Langlaagte in 1886, less than 100 years ago. As the scale of gold deposits became apparent, Johannesburg became the nineteenth century's last great boom town, and changed the face of South Africa from an agricultural society to the largest producer of gold in the world.

Enjoying a sandwich and a fruit drink on a park bench outside the City Hall, we find ourselves seated beside an elderly gentleman, a Mr Van Rooyen, who is delighted to answer our many questions. He tells us the gold rush brought thousands of people searching for good fortune, and so Johannesburg was born. Originally no more than a mining camp, it grew and it grew.

'The tents and the clay huts are long gone,' he says, 'But as you can see,' he points at the cityscape surrounding us. 'The buildings that replaced them are a bit of a hodge podge. I guess this reflects rapid growth. Still, there are many grand buildings.'

We spend the afternoon with this dear man, who is a fount of knowledge, viewing the mining houses and the Chamber of Mines, and then we take him for afternoon tea. One thing that strikes me is the dearth of black people. I've already learnt that whites only constitute about fifteen per cent of the population, so I can't help wondering where all the black people are.

'I can see you have a lot to learn, Mona,' Mr Van Rooyen says. 'Johannesburg is very much a white city. Black people live in townships on the outskirts of the city. They can come in to work, but have to carry what is known as a "pass".'

I'm a bit puzzled by this, and actually quite outraged by a system that can keep most of the population out of the city. But nonetheless, I'm determined to find out more about what apartheid means for the people living here.

Plenty of building is underway and high-rise skyscrapers seem to have taken over the inner city. 'Looks like there's plenty of work for me,' says Iain,' but first we'll get ourselves settled, and then I'll see what Samorgan has in mind.'

One evening on our rounds, we pass a pub, from which loud music is blaring. Peeping in through the open door we see couples dancing, but in a style we've never seen before. The couples advance, each partner with an arm held straight out in front, hands clasped. The music, too, sounds strange to my ears.

'It sounds like Scottish Country Dance music gone

wrong.' Iain, ever the music man, laughs heartily.

We learn later that this is the traditional music of the Afrikaners. It's called *boeremusiek* – the music of the farmers – and the dance is known as 'lang arm', or long arm. It seems very odd to my ear and eye, but Iain points out that South Africans would probably find the sight of Scottish men dancing in tartan kilts just as strange.

We are surprised to be feeling sad about leaving the Pelican. It's not the hotel we'll miss – heaven forbid – but the folk we have met there: immigrants from the UK and Ireland, and South Africans too, black and white. One jovial black woman called Grace, who keeps our bedroom clean, asks me to let her come to our flat, once we've moved.

'I'll do your washing and ironing, and cleaning too, Madam.'

I feel decidedly awkward at being addressed as Madam but, after numerous unsuccessful attempts to make her stop, I have reluctantly become used to it. I tell Grace that I'd like to settle in first, but take a number on which I can reach her.

It's time for our farewells, with promises of meeting up again, and then we're off on the next leg of our adventure. The flat is ready and waiting and all we have to do is carry in our luggage. We collect the key from the caretaker and in we go to a bright, small, clean abode. Iain picks me up and carries me across the threshold into our first South African home. I'm no lightweight, and we collapse on the sofa laughing our heads off.

We recover, and start unpacking. But Iain soon loses interest and wanders out onto the balcony. He gives a shout. 'Come here and have a look, it's the Hillbrow Tower.' And there it is in all its glory. We have seen it from ground level but, from our balcony, it's so close we're sure that, if we throw a pebble, we could hit it easily.

Iain has, of course, already read all about it, so he is not only fascinated to see it, but happy to fill me in. 'Construction started on the tower last year ... it's a Posts and Telecommunications build. It's supposed to be 269 metres high, which means it'll be the tallest structure in the country, with a revolving restaurant at the top – imagine that.'

When it comes to research, I'm always surprised by how thorough Iain is, and how enthusiastic he is about everything. I've got an eager guidebook on tap.

At the end of our week of exploring, Iain has an interview with Murray and Roberts, a multinational engineering and construction company. Much to my relief, all goes well.

'I'm impressed with my new employers,' Iain tells me after his meeting. 'They're friendly and accommodating and they even expressed interest in you.'

I can see Iain is pleased, and I'm chuffed. He'll start work in the first week of November, which gives us another week's holiday. Time to explore the bright lights of Hillbrow.

***

'Do you think this one will do?' Iain asks. We are in a second-hand car dealership, somewhere in Hillbrow. He's pointing at a yellow Volkswagen Beetle, a bit tired looking, and not really my cup of tea.

'Okay, let's take it for a test drive.' I suppress a sigh. I'm a bit fed up with trailing around looking at cars, but I try to be chirpy.

By eleven o'clock, we are the owners of a very cheap, very old, very worn-out Beetle. It is far from being a dream car, but we don't have a great deal of money to spare and, as long as it doesn't let us down, it will serve its purpose.

Hillbrow is a vibrant, thriving cosmopolitan suburb. There is a building boom going on, so Iain tells me, and he should know after his interview with Murray and Roberts. Everywhere we look, more and more high-rise buildings are going up. We love watching the African men at work. Music is in their blood and, working as a team, they sing and sometimes dance. We stand and watch, and are rewarded by broad smiles. I marvel at such unaffected friendliness towards white strangers, considering the conditions under which they live and work.

We are astonished by the impossibly heavy burdens that African women carry on their heads, often with babies on their backs. And not just their own babies. I was fascinated to see a white baby boy, blond curls bobbing, squealing and laughing on his nanny's back. It made me wonder if she had her own children, and where they might be, and at the sadness she must surely be feeling at raising someone else's children rather than her own.

For the rest of the holiday week, we go on the prowl around Hillbrow. Magda and Tina, two South African students, share a flat next door. They are young and full of life, and we have become friends. They have offered to show us the sights and sounds of Hillbrow.

The suburb is full of European immigrants from the UK and Ireland, Greece, Portugal, Italy, Germany, Holland, Australia and New Zealand, together with a fair sprinkling of South Africans. The inhabitants are almost entirely white – although Africans live in rooms on the tops of many of the buildings. They are the "flat boys" who clean and service the blocks of high-rise apartments.

I don't know where our two new friends get their

energy, considering they are at college, and need their sleep, but happily they provide us with guided tours of the area, which is dense with book and record shops, with live music venues and dance clubs, like the Chelsea Hotel, with its crystal chandeliers and the Summit Club for dancing. There's even an Irish Club, which specialises in folk music. Iain plays both the fiddle and the mandolin and, when one of the Irish lads hands him a fiddle, he gives a grand performance, which is applauded by the boisterous crowd. In fact, he's such a hit that he's invited to join the resident band on Friday nights.

'They've offered to pay me too,' he tells me. I can see excitement in his eyes. 'It'll help get us that new car ... maybe.'

The highlight is being taken by Magda and Tina to see a stripper called Glenda Kemp, who has scandalised the country by dancing provocatively, wearing nothing but a thong – and her snake Oupa. She is very good but, halfway through, I have seen as much as I can take, and the snake gives me the heebie jeebies. I plead a headache and beg off.

I do like the South African accents, both Afrikaans and English. Tina and Magda put on a show for us in order to teach us local slang and Iain and I laugh until our sides are sore. We learn that the word 'shame' covers a multitude of sins, including empathy and just plain 'cuteness'. We also have to get our heads around the fact that 'just now' doesn't mean 'now', but sometime in the future. Tina and Magda teach us to swear in Afrikaans, and laugh uproariously when I find these words more exotic and somehow nicer than their English equivalents.

Shops are plentiful in the two main streets of Hillbrow, Pretoria and Kotze Streets, including jewellery shops, with windows filled with beautiful South African gold and diamond rings, bracelets and necklaces.

The food is excellent, and well within our budget. We sample tender T-bone steaks, Italian and Portuguese food and, when we find ourselves still up and ravenous in the wee small hours, we make for the popular Fontana Bakery, famous for its juicy barbecue chicken.

But sightseeing is interesting for only so long. Towards the end of our holiday, I find myself champing at the bit. I want to get stuck into a job again. I raise the matter over a coffee on the balcony of Café Wien. 'Perhaps wait for the new year,' Iain says. Well, maybe he's right. But there's no reason for me not to do a little research in the meantime.

I get a list of local hospitals and have a good look to see what's on offer. There's the Johannesburg General Hospital, the Fever Hospital, The Queen Victoria Maternity Hospital and the Transvaal Memorial Hospital for Children. These are all government hospitals for white folk. The Hillbrow Hospital is for black people. Then there are private hospitals and clinics, for those who can afford private care, and have medical insurance, like the Brenthurst and Princess Alice. The Florence Nightingale and the Lady Dudley and more. I shut my eyes and take a stab at the list. I seem to have chosen the Brenthurst.

I'm surprised when, after a chat with the matron on the telephone, she says, 'If you're not doing anything in particular today, why don't you come along and see me.'

***

Matron Bell is an imposing woman in her early forties, I'm guessing, in a dark green uniform and a starched white frilly hat. She has a kind face and a friendly smile, and puts me at ease immediately. I've brought all my qualification papers with me, and I'm able to assure her that I'm registered with the South African Nursing Council – I made sure of that before leaving Scotland.

Matron Bell is very thorough and we spend a good hour together. She picks up one of my qualifications.

'I'm interested to see you have a health visitor qualification. I know the health department is keen to recruit health visitors. It seems they have a shortage. I would certainly employ you, but perhaps you could give the health visitor option some thought.'

I tell Matron Bell that I would certainly like to pursue all the options and she immediately lifts the phone and speaks to a Miss Clark at the city health department, who is in charge of health visitor recruitment and training. Matron Bell's face is animated and she mentions my name repeatedly.

'Sister McAlpine arrived from Scotland a fortnight ago. Yes, she's registered and has reference letters. I'll ask her.' She turns to me. 'Miss Clark is very interested to meet you. She suggests 9am tomorrow?'

CHAPTER THREE
Diving in the deep end

November 1969

'That's one of the many things I love you for, Mo,' says Iain, 'I never do know what you'll be up to next. But I do worry.'

It's a hot and sultry night. We're sitting cross-legged on the floor of our flat, stark naked, except for bath towels wrung out in cold water, and strategically slung around our shoulders. Every window is fully open in the hope of capturing whatever cool air might be passing by outside.

'I know it's the heat, but I also know your restlessness has more to do with your impending chat with Miss Clark, so I know you're anxious about it. What's the hurry?'

He's right. Since my spontaneous agreement to the appointment, I've been in turmoil. I'm excited, but also apprehensive. And Iain's concern is affecting me.

'Maybe a post in a white hospital would be a safer option to start with?' he asks me gently. He leans forward and kisses the top of my head.

Maybe I am being stupid, plunging into communities I know nothing about. Will I be any help to them? And perhaps I'll be putting myself needlessly in danger through my ignorance and naïveté. There's no way I'll be able to sleep tonight. I look at Iain helplessly.

'You don't have to take the job. In fact, you don't need to rush. Give it some thought.'

***

It's nine o' clock, and I'm all scrubbed up on the outside, with a racing heart on the inside.

Miss Clark, bless her, puts me at ease. I have to admit a strong coffee helps. She's a small, wizened woman, who greets me with warmth in her austere, utilitarian office.

We get to the crux of the matter immediately. She tells me she has me in mind for a clinic on the edge of Johannesburg's largest black township, Soweto. She looks at me expectantly and lights a cigarette.

In that instant, I make up my mind. 'Safe options are not for me, Miss Clark, I'm going to give it a go, come what may.'

Miss Clark takes a deep drag on her cigarette, squinting through the stream of smoke. 'Noordgesig is, of course, a coloured clinic. But I'm confident that you'll warm to the coloureds, as they will to you.'

She breaks into a hacking cough which racks her whole body. I wait for her to recover, wondering whether I can ask the question uppermost in my mind. I'm confused by the term 'coloured', but am wary to show my ignorance. Before I can question her further, she takes a breath and rushes on.

'I'm glad to hear you're taking the post. I appreciate that it's a challenge, but I'm here for you and will give you full support. It's good you have a car.'

Oh no, the car! I don't tell her that Iain and I have to wrangle with each other for use of the Yellow Peril. And she's sure to sack me on the spot once she claps her eyes on my sorry excuse for transport.

'You'll start the first of December.' With that, she smiles

and gives me a hearty handshake.

Meantime, I'm crossing my fingers behind my back and praying Yellow Peril will not let me down. 'And by the way, you do realise you'll be sister in charge of the clinic?'

Oh well, in for a penny, in for a pound.

***

'Good news,' Iain tells me, bounding through the door from his first day at work. He has a big grin on his face. 'They've given me a bakkie.'

'What on earth is a bakkie?'

'It's the South African word for a pick-up. Now we're a two-car family.'

Things seem to be falling into place. At least the Beetle will be mine and mine alone, as long as it doesn't break down. But now there's another hurdle: finding the Noordgesig Clinic, with my pathetic sense of direction.

Luckily, Iain allays my fears on both scores. Thanks to his knowledge of mechanics, the car is going like a bomb. And, sensing my other anxiety, he takes my hand and smiles.

'How about we take a drive there this weekend? That way, you can learn the route before you start.'

So, on a bright blue Saturday morning – I'm still enthralled by the African sky – we're on our way.

West, we go along Empire Road, then past Auckland Park and the pretty suburb of Westdene. On our left is the big JG Strydom Hospital, and on our right the white suburb of Triomf. I've been reading about this suburb, so we slow down to see it properly. It has a fascinating, and tragic history that nearly broke my heart when I learnt the details.

This area was once known as Sophiatown, a mixed

suburb, which became the epicentre of black politics, jazz and blues music, producing some of South Africa's most famous writers, musicians and artists.

Then on the 9 February 1955, apartheid South Africa moved in and destroyed the area, forcibly removing 60 000 residents. Rising out of the rubble, Triomf became a new white suburb. Ironically triomf is the Afrikaans word for triumph.

Next, we drive on past Coronation Hospital, which I was told serves 'Coloured' people. On we go, passing great mine dumps, relics of the gold rush of the last century.

At last, we're on the brow of a hill that leads down to Noordgesig. I note green veld and a river. And then on our right is the clinic, the very first building in Soweto.

The road to the clinic is bumpy, but Yellow Peril seems to take it in her stride. Iain turns off the engine and we sit for a bit, taking in our surroundings.

For a building that houses a primary health clinic, an antenatal clinic, a family planning clinic and a child health and baby clinic, it seems a bit on the small side. We prowl around the building, but there's no one about and all is quiet. Miss Clark has informed me that the clinic closes over the weekend. There are midwives on call, but those in need of other health services travel to Coronation Hospital.

I decide that I've seen enough for one day and I'll leave the rest until I take up my post. A memory comes flooding back of my first day on Fair Isle. I remember how nervous I was, and how I was on the verge of giving up. I mention this to Iain.

'I'm glad you soldiered on back then,' he says with a chuckle. 'It was good training for what you might well be faced with in Noordgesig. At least here you'll have a doctor for backup.'

It's not that I'm so worried about, I tell Iain. I feel comfortable with my duties. 'It's just that I'm a bit puzzled about the term "coloured". Miss Clark was quite comfortable using the term but I know that, in America, it holds derogatory connotations. I'm not sure what it means and what terms to use. I wish I'd discussed this with her.'

Iain steps in front of me and lays his hands on my shoulders. 'You'll find all this out quickly enough, once you start. You know you're on a steep learning curve. I know you: you're scared of causing offence. But my advice would be to ask, ask and ask again. I'm certainly going to do that. We have such a lot to learn and we're on an exciting journey, let's enjoy the ride.'

No sooner are we on our way back to Jo'burg than four barefoot boys appear out of nowhere, kicking up the dust and throwing a ball around. They give us huge smiles, wave and shout farewell in what we take to be Afrikaans.

'You see, Mo, they love you already,' Iain says with smile. We wave back enthusiastically and I'm hopeful that the rest of the Noordgesig residents will be as welcoming.

***

December 1969

A week before my first big Noordgesig day, I decide to call on Grace and invite her to our flat. I like her, and have decided to take her on to help me with our washing and ironing.

She arrives on my doorstep with her big smile and even bigger personality. I lead her to our tiny sitting room area, but she is clearly too uncomfortable to sit with me there. Instead, we perch on our kitchen stools, where she seems more at ease.

I broach the subject of a job and she is thrilled. 'I really do need this job. I work at the hotel full time, but I can come on my day off.'

I feel terrible now and feel my face flushing. How insensitive of me. 'Oh no, Grace, you need a day off to rest, surely?'

She shakes her head vigorously and looks worried, clearly concerned that I may withdraw the offer. 'I have two school-going children who live with my mother in Soweto. I always need extra money.'

'Well then, if you're sure, the job's yours if you want it.'

I rise to switch the kettle on, but she is immediately beside me, wresting it from my hand and carrying it to the sink.

'Thank you so much, Madam, you've made my life much easier.'

She's used that word again – madam – and again I'm left with a feeling of discomfort.

Shop assistants and cleaners in our block of flats have continued to address me as Madam but, for a more intimate working relationship, it sounds strange and, again, I explain my misgivings to her.

She gives a resounding laugh. 'It's just the way it is. I'd feel very funny not to be calling you Madam.'

She orients herself quickly in our kitchenette, edges me out of the way and takes over the tea-making. I'm not used to that either, but I am impressed by her eagerness.

Left with nothing to do, I awkwardly sink back onto my stool.

The afternoon wears on and I start feeling more comfortable with Grace. She is highly intelligent and I ask her about her schooling. She explains that she had to leave school at age 16, in Standard 8, because her mother was in need of financial support. Her father had abandoned them years before. 'And in any case, I was pregnant.'

She takes a sip of her tea, very strong, I notice, with a great deal of sugar. I decide to take Iain's advice and 'ask, ask, ask'. And who better to ask than this woman. I ask about the term 'coloured', and how it's used.

'Well, you see, you are white and I'm black, and then we have people whose blood is mixed, maybe a black mother and a white father. They don't know who they are!'

I am amused, but I'm not quite sure how to take that. I decide not to press her on this point, but rather to move on. 'I'm going to work in Noordgesig Clinic. Do you know it?'

She finishes her tea and stands immediately, carrying it to the sink. 'Oh yes, I know Noordgesig. My home is in the next township of Orlando. The coloureds are really nice and you'll like them.' She gives her cup a last wipe with the dish cloth, turns and smiles at me.

I sincerely hope so.

I'm seriously tempted to ask Grace about her feelings and thoughts about apartheid, but I zip my lip, thinking that's a step too far. Sorry, Iain, I'm not ready to cross that line, not yet at any rate. We chat for a couple of hours and I ask more about her children and her mother.

I can tell that she is surprised by my interest and that makes me sad, that no one has thought to talk to her about her life before.

We agree that Grace will work for me every Saturday.

CHAPTER FOUR
A different world

December 1969

I'm feeling more than a little apprehensive as I drive out to Noordgesig on a beautiful summer's day. First day in a brand-new job, and second month in a brand-new country. I smile at my thoughts. The traffic is thick and so is my head, I didn't sleep a wink last night.

I give myself a shake and a good talking to and by the time Noordgesig Clinic comes into view I'm determined to make the most of it and I cheer up considerably.

I park Yellow Peril under the shade of a gnarled old tree near the entrance of the clinic and a young man in a white coat appears almost immediately to greet me.

'Hello, you must be Sister McAlpine?' He takes my hand in introduction. 'I'm Dr Sol. I'm happy to meet you.'

I do like the look of this friendly, smiling young man. He's about my age, or maybe in his early thirties. 'I must confess, I'm a bit anxious about taking on this job.'

He ushers me towards the entrance. 'Don't you worry. I'll help you settle in. We work as a team here so, in no time, you'll learn the ropes. The staff is excited to meet you.'

With that, Dr Sol guides me into a clinic room in which fifteen or so staff members are waiting. I'm aware of the fact that they're sizing me up – although I'm relieved to see that some are smiling.

I take a quick glance around and see four well-dressed young men standing to one side. I'm introduced to the nearest of them, whose name is Sidley.

'Pleased to meet you, Sister. I'm Sidley, senior in administration.' I note the kind, open face. 'This is Sam, Thomas, and Solly, the chaps that keep me right.'

I note that Sidley's skin is pale brown, Sam and Thomas are very dark, and Solly is a shade in between. I'm intrigued. What on earth constitutes coloured? Not the time to ask, Mo, I tell myself. No doubt I'll find out in due course.

Through the handshakes that ensue, Thomas is the only one who doesn't smile. He gives me a sideways look and I feel an undercurrent of dislike. I tell myself I'm imagining things and try hard to dismiss my gut feeling. I do wish he'd smile, though.

Next, it's the nursing staff. Ten are qualified in general nursing and midwifery and two hold health visitor qualifications.

We shake hands and, one by one, they tell me their names. They are all relaxed and friendly, which is a relief. It's quite a lot to take in at one fell swoop but I'm determined as time goes on to get to know each one personally.

Finally, Abel, the cleaner and general handyman, takes my hand and gives me a huge, toothy smile. He's a talkative fellow and I'm shocked when he tells me that he's in his mid-thirties. He looks over fifty. His emaciated body and skull-like face surely have a tale to tell.

It's clear he's led a tough life and, after close questioning, I learn that he was orphaned at an early age, and largely neglected by other family members. Despite the obvious neglect, he has a smiling face and tells me how happy he is working in the clinic.

Sister Rosie, one of the senior nurses, has taken it upon herself to hand over to me. Rosie is large and round and has an intimidating way about her. I'll need to watch myself around her. A woman in her mid-forties, she is logical and knowledgeable, as well as efficient.

The clinic is already filling up with patients. Rosie informs me that for the next couple of hours it's going to be very busy, but a formal meeting with the staff has been arranged for mid-morning. She's advised me to make a speech introducing myself. 'It will help the staff get to know you, Sister McAlpine.'

I realise I'll do well to take Rosie's advice. She clearly knows best. Forewarned that I'm to be in charge, I've had plenty of time to think about my approach. Nevertheless, when it comes time for me to make my speech, I'm hoping that my vulnerability doesn't show.

I start my story by telling them who I am and where I'm from, and about my short spell in South Africa. I have had a look at the list of staff names and ages, so I know that most are older than me. I make a point of greeting every one of them by name.

'I know that I'm younger than most of you, but I've had a good training in all aspects of the nursing skills required to be in charge of this clinic. What I don't have, and what you have, is years of experience, especially in the midwifery field. I have no intention of sitting in my office ticking the boxes. I want to learn from you, I'm hoping I can work alongside you, and that you will teach me.'

My eyes scan the faces before me, and rest on Sister Hilda, one of the younger nurses. 'What do you say, Sister Hilda, would you be willing to take me on?'

There is a burst of laughter from the group as Hilda

looks around. A flush shows through the coffee-coloured skin of her pretty face.

'Oh, my goodness, I don't know if I can, I don't have the experience of Maud and Anna. Maybe you should ask them, but if you think I'll be all right, then, yes, I would be very willing.'

'Well, that's that, then. I'm very happy to work with you all as a team so that we can learn from each other. Speak with me privately if any of you have any questions, my door is always open. Tomorrow, I'll work on the general side but, if there's a midwifery call-out, I'd like to come along.'

I spend the rest of the day attending to administration. Sister Rosie joins me and we have a long chat and a catch-up. I tell her I don't speak Afrikaans, the language of the coloured people throughout South Africa and ask her if this will put me at a disadvantage.

'Not at all, we can all speak English. There are two official languages, so take your pick.'

'I can see, Sister Rosie, that I'm going to have to call on you to keep me right. I hope I can learn quickly.'

'I'll be your right-hand woman,' she says. Her eyes sparkle and her mouth turns up in a beautiful smile. I'm glad to see that smile. Her face, in repose, has a solemn, rather dour look. 'I can see that the staff is a bit taken aback by your attitude. This is South Africa, Sister McAlpine. We're not used to white people making us feel important. You're treating us with respect and dignity. Thank you.'

Well, I never would have believed it, I tell myself on my way home. How on earth can anyone who is in the privileged position of being in charge of people, not treat them with dignity and respect? I have no intention of changing my ways, apartheid or not.

***

By the time I report for duty on day two, the waiting area is full. Young men, old men, mothers with babies on their laps and toddlers by their sides, teenagers and grannies are all waiting their turn to see a nurse or doctor.

I notice a concerned woman holding a baby, who looks limp and ill. I report this to Dr Sol.

'Bring them in immediately,' he says. 'Let them jump the queue, I'll take a look.'

The baby is three months old and the mother tells us that he became hot and drowsy during the night and refused all feeds. I'm touched to see how gentle Sol is with both baby and mom. They converse in Afrikaans and I listen carefully, trying to make head or tail of it, telling myself I must learn the language.

Baby Craig's temperature is 40 degrees, there is a pronounced rash over his body, and he's dehydrated. He's making whimpering sounds as he breathes.

Dr Sol looks at me with pursed lips and a frown, and nods. I instinctively know he suspects meningitis. He tells mom that her baby is very sick and needs to go to Coronation Hospital. I offer to look after baby Craig while his mom rushes home. Her sister has a car. In under half an hour, baby Craig is off to nearby Coro, as the hospital is known.

It was a dramatic start to the day, and I vow to keep tabs on the family and find out what happens to the little mite. I do hope he makes it, but my heart is filled with fear. My own baby sister died of meningitis in the Fifties, and the disease still fills me with dread.

I gradually come to grips with Noordgesig Clinic. Over the weeks that follow, I fall into a routine. I join the nursing staff each morning to hear their reports and go through the work schedule for the day. After lunch I go to my office and attend to phone calls and administration.

On Wednesday morning, I decide to join Sister Rachel, one of the health visitors, in the baby clinic. Moms with babies are already milling around joking and laughing, waiting their turn to have their babies weighed and checked, and enjoying some social interaction with one another. It's a relaxed time and, because there are a number of feeding problems, I ask Rachel if I can give a talk about breast and bottle-feeding. She agrees. I'm heartened to hear that most moms breastfeed and I encourage this.

They laugh when I tell them I have an English-to-Afrikaans phrase book and have been practising. They tell me not to worry. If I'm stuck, they are happy to *'praat in Engels'*.

One very young mom clasps her breasts and looks at me appealingly. *'Suster my borste is vol en pynlik. Moet ek ophou met borsvoeding en gee my baba mos 'n bottel?'*

I try to work this out. I recognise *bors* for breast, *pynlik* for pain, *vol* for full and, of course, *'bottel'*.

I walk over and lay a hand on her shoulder. 'No, you're doing great. Baby is gaining weight beautifully. Let me explain what I think you should do.'

I'm rewarded with a clapping of hands and a shout from one of the moms. *'Suster is baie slim, sy kan Afrikaans praat.'*

I recognise from my phrase book that they're saying I'm clever because I can speak Afrikaans. I must admit that I'm chuffed to bits, and promise myself again to learn the language.

***

The clinic closes over Christmas and New Year, when Coronation Hospital will take over responsibility for all medical concerns. The clinic staff is looking forward to a break, and I am too, as is Iain. The building industry also shuts down at this time.

By the last day before the holidays, I'm happy with my progress and I'm learning as I go along. I'm in my office writing up off-duty rosters and filling in statistics when I hear a loud scream. It seems to be coming from outside, so I leap up and rush to the main entrance. A woman is doubled up in pain in the driveway.

It takes me no time to work out that she's in labour and that, if I don't do something very quickly, I'll have to deliver her baby right there.

I kneel beside her and I can see that there's nothing for it but to pick her up and carry her into the clinic. Fortunately, aside from her large tummy, she is small and slight.

'Now then, not to worry, your baby is on the way. Try and stay calm. I'm right here with you, and nothing bad is going to happen.' Her eyes plead with me as she holds fast to my arm.

By this time, a crowd has gathered and the woman is screaming and pushing, and it's taking me all my time to calm the situation down. I notice people backing off, and I'm sure it's because they're concerned that I might ask them to take on my burden.

It's a hot day and I stagger into the clinic, sweating profusely. I think quickly, then carry her through to my office. It's the one place we can guarantee privacy. I lay her gently on the floor. The other midwives have run to join me by this stage and we all cluster about her. We pack cushions around her and cover her with a blanket. It's clear this baby is determined to make its appearance within minutes.

Adrenaline floods my body, but I don't have time to feel nervous. I turn to the midwives. 'Can I deliver the baby?'

They nod and I turn back to the young mother, grateful for their support behind me.

I ask her name. 'Now, don't you worry, Adele,' I croon. 'Just relax. You're safe now. I can see the baby's head already, so when you're ready, give us a good push.'

Two big pushes and Adele Van Wyk delivers herself of a handsome 3.5kg baby boy.

Up to now, I've been entirely focused on Adele. As I wrap her baby in the towel one of the midwives has produced, I become aware of a hubbub behind me. I turn and find that a party atmosphere has developed in my office. Everyone is clapping and laughing.

I gladly turn Adele over to the midwives, but she has bonded with me. 'Thank you, thank you Sister,' she says over and over. 'Baie dankie, I was terrified that I wasn't going to make it to the clinic.'

Once Adele is all cleaned up, I bathe baby Van Wyk and wrap him in a big warm bath towel, hand him over to his mom and watch, as I've done many times, the delight on a new mother's face; that look of awe. I can feel a lump rise in my throat and a tear in my eye. It's her first baby and she tells me that she intends to breastfeed.

'That's great. Would you like me to help you latch him on to your breast?'

She nods and it doesn't take much – he's more than ready for his first feed. He suckles hungrily and a tear trickles on to Adele's cheek. The midwives cheer.

Sister Rosie and I decide we'll take her home in my car. Noordgesig is a relatively small suburb, so most homes are within walking distance of the clinic. Adele's husband is at work so we collect her mother along the way. Rosie reassures them that, although she'll be on holiday, she'll pop in and visit.

The party atmosphere still prevails when Rosie and I get back. Oros orange juice cordial takes pride of place. And Hilda has been busy baking.

'I've made koeksusters,' she tells me, which I learn are fried pastries, crisp and syrup-soaked on the outside, soft and moist at their centre. They're delicious. I make a little speech, thanking them for their support and friendship and for making me feel loved and welcome. Then I again shake each hand and wish them a happy Christmas and all the best for 1970.

CHAPTER FIVE

Painful lessons

.

Letters and Christmas cards are filling our flat and we read, sometimes with tear-filled eyes, news of home from family and friends. I'm feeling very homesick. I know Iain is too, although he won't admit it. We've made friends, mostly with fellow immigrants, and much time is spent in each other's company. Iain's musical background has guaranteed friendships with fellow musicians and, on many an evening, we enjoy informal parties in our homes with a Scottish/Irish band on tap.

On Christmas day, Patsy and Ian Mundie, our Shetland friends, have invited us to their home.

It's a strange day. We awake to a blistering Jo'burg and I feel disorientated.

'Not exactly a Shetland Christmas, is it? Our folks will be battling the wind and the snow and, no doubt, they're freezing, while we're here in Africa sweating and roasting. I'm not sure I can get used to this, it's so very different.'

I frown at my token gesture for the season: the small Christmas tree and the figure of a tiny Santa that I've set up on our dresser.

'I'm sure he's winking at you, Mo. Come on, let's get ready for our visit.'

Their excited kids, Julie and Sean, greet us

enthusiastically and show us what Santa has left for them. We're duly impressed and spend time admiring the dolls and cars and playing card games with them.

'We're thrilled you're here,' says Patsy. 'I hope you'll enjoy the dinner. We don't do turkey and trimmings, it's far too hot to slave over a hot stove. Come outside. Ian is busy lighting the braai.'

Braai? I've heard of it and I know that it's the Afrikaans word for barbecue, but I've never seen or experienced one, so I'm intrigued.

The coals are glowing and the table is groaning with all kinds of salads and bottles of South African wine.

'South Africans are very precious about their braais,' Ian tells us. 'We never refer to them as barbecues. It isn't a braai if it's cooked over a gas grill. It's a social occasion too, and we keep the fire going for the duration. Even after we've eaten, we'll sit around the fire and spend the rest of the day chatting and drinking and having a good time.'

He hands Iain a pair of braai tongs. 'There you are, I'll make a South African of you yet. Let's get the boerewors going.' They laugh and joke together while enjoying a dram or two of Scotland's finest malt whisky, and in no time at all the wonderful smell of the wood smoke and cooking meat is causing our mouths to water in anticipation.

The braai meat is simply delicious. We tuck in until our tummies are ready to burst, but we forgot about the Highveld storm that kicks in most summer afternoons at around five o'clock.

Ian's prepared for the storm, though, and lifts the garage door.

'Give me a hand,' he tells Iain. Together they lift the portable braai and place it inside, near the open door. We just manage to drag our chairs undercover when the heavens open. The rain is torrential. Lightning shoots from the heavens and thunder blasts at our eardrums. It's dramatic and a little frightening. Then, just as suddenly, the show comes to an end. Within minutes, the air clears and the world is clean and steaming. Back the braai goes to its original spot and we follow.

The evening settles in with much laughing and reminiscing about our previous lives in Shetland. Patsy is great fun and I can tell that I've made a firm friend. As we thank the Mundie's for our terrific first South African Christmas, and their kind hospitality, we promise more visits, outings, and shopping trips.

'No, that's not good enough,' says Iain. 'It's New Year celebrations next week. Let's get together for Hogmanay. Our flat is so tiny and we don't want to disturb the neighbours. I've promised to play at the Irish Club until 2am when we'll bring in the UK New Year. What do you think? Would you join us?'

'We'd love that,' Ian exclaims. 'We'll get a baby sitter and we'll certainly be there. Hogmanay is such a Scottish institution; we have to celebrate it.'

On our way home, we notice how empty the city feels. Most of Johannesburg, it seems, the white residents, anyway, decamps to the coast for the summer holidays. It feels strange still being here, driving these empty roads. What will we do for the coming week, I wonder aloud? Iain has obviously also been thinking. He immediately comes up with the idea of a trip.

'How about Durban?'

I'm doubtful. 'Do you think the Yellow Peril will get us there?'

'We'll hire a car. What do you say?'

'Let's do it,' I say impulsively.

'I've been doing a bit of research.' Iain is looking decidedly sheepish. 'The flat and the heat have been getting me down a bit, so I made a few enquiries. There's a car hire place in Jules Street that's open tomorrow.'

***

By nine the next day, with a couple of bags packed and ensconced in a very comfortable car, we're off to Durban. We open the car windows and enjoy the cool air and the sense of freedom of being on the open road.

We reach Van Reenen's Pass by lunchtime, and stop for a bite to eat before resuming our journey down the high majestic pass that winds its way through the Drakensberg Mountains. This is by far my favourite part of the drive.

In my vivid imagination, I can see the intrepid voortrekkers struggling up these impossible paths and roads in their covered wagons, making for the interior of South Africa.

It's quite a journey, but we've both enjoyed every mile, and it's given us another view of our adopted country. We make for the centre of Durban and, as the blue water of the Indian Ocean comes into sight, I catch my breath, realising how much I've missed the sea.

We're very lucky to find a room in a comfortable hotel on the waterfront and we book in for four nights. We get our heads down and go to sleep to the sound of waves. Bliss.

For the next week, we don't venture far from the beach and spend our time sunbathing and swimming in the sea.

We are fascinated by the rickshaws, three-wheeled tuk-tuks pulled along by local Zulu men, wearing magnificent head dresses, adorned with beads and ornamental decorations. It's such fun going for rickshaw rides along the beachfront, passing the locals, selling their crafts and wares from impromptu stalls.

There are no black or coloured people on the beach, so I ask the Indian waiter who serves us breakfast, why this is.

'Only white people are allowed on the beaches,' he says. He's figured out we're not from South Africa. 'We Indians are not allowed either.'

He introduces himself as Mohammad and, once he sees we're interested, he opens up and explains that there are four racial groups in South Africa: black, white, coloured and Asian. I feel a bit stupid that I didn't know this already. He goes on to tell us about the large community of Indians in Durban.

'In fact, Durban is regarded as the largest Indian city outside of India. We are mostly the descendants of indentured workers. They were brought to Natal to work in the sugar cane industry. If you like curry, I'll recommend some good Indian restaurants for you to try.'

We take his advice. Iain loves curry, and declares these to be some of the finest curries he's tasted, but I'm a bit of a baby about too much spice.

On our last day in Durban, we decide to take an early walk on the beach. It's 7am and there's hardly a soul around except for some folk in the far distance. We stroll along the promenade, hand in hand, relishing the fresh, sea breeze.

Passing a park bench, I notice something which, at first, I take to be a bundle of tattered clothing. As we draw near, it becomes apparent that the 'bundle' is a sleeping black man. He reeks of alcohol and body odour.

The next instant, a police van screeches to a halt. A policeman bolts from the van and lays into the man. He drags him from beneath the bench and proceeds to punch and kick him.

He drags the poor man to his feet. I can't understand a

word he's saying, but I recognise 'fok' and 'kaffir', which I know to be extremely offensive words.

I am incensed and aghast, and run forward. 'Stop it,' I yell. 'Stop beating him like that.'

The policeman turns and glares at me. Iain, bless him, pulls me back. 'He's a policeman, Mo. Leave it, otherwise we'll also end up in that van.'

I'm in tears by this time, which seems to amuse the policeman. He gives a curt laugh, then launches a great glob of spit on the ground in front of me.

That's just too much for Iain. He strides up to this horrible guy and, with his left hand, grabs the policeman's right wrist. With his right hand, he grabs and squeezes the policeman's left wrist, causing him to let go of his victim.

I stand rooted to the ground while Iain threatens to punch his opponent in the face. 'I don't care if you take me to the police station, what you're doing to this poor man is despicable.'

I'm in shock, and I stand paralysed. Iain is a strong man and, once riled, he can easily injure an opponent. I see that the policeman has a gun on his belt. I don't dare think what could happen next. I hold my breath.

The next instant, the police officer steps back. I can't believe my eyes. He backed down. Still shouting and swearing, his face a bright shade of red, he flounders around, before hauling his poor victim to his feet.

The drunk guy is staggering and apologising. 'Sorry baas, sorry baas,' he keeps repeating. This seems to enrage the policeman even more. He continues to drag and push the man up on to the road, then throws him into his van.

I find my voice. 'Oh, Iain, I'm so proud of you.'

'Not the first bully I've had to deal with,' he says, breathing heavily. 'A coward will always cave in when confronted.'

A small crowd has gathered to see what all the commotion is. An elderly man asks Iain what's going on. He looks at me anxiously while Iain gives a quick summary.

'You did what?' a young woman bursts out. 'You're mad, you know. You could have been locked up for assaulting a policeman.'

'So be it,' Iain says with a wry smile. He takes my hand and we walk away from the appalling incident that has destroyed the enjoyment of our last day.

Back in the car, we catch our breath, I become a little hysterical and let out an inappropriate laugh. 'I'm not sure if I want to stay in this country, Iain, never mind another holiday in Durban.'

'Now calm down, Mo, let's go for a coffee. We'll make decisions once we're back home in Jo'burg.

CHAPTER SIX
Doubt

January 1970

After all the excitement of settling down in South Africa, I feel deflated. The dreadful incident on the Durban beachfront has affected me more than I care to admit, even to myself. I'm trying hard to keep my good humour for Iain's sake, but I'm not enjoying life. I kept a smile on my face while bringing in the New Year with our friends at the Irish Club.

But now, the time for starting work again is drawing near and I still haven't recovered. I'm emotionally drained, and I'm feeling anxious.

The 'nurse' in me is telling me that I'm depressed. I know that I should be talking about my feelings. Keeping them inside is not healthy. But who do I go to for help? A doctor maybe?

Nah! I'll keep going. Next week Monday I'll be back at Noordgesig. Perhaps I'll feel better once I'm busy again. I decide to wait and see.

But waiting and seeing doesn't seem to be working.

Early on Friday morning, I wake up in tears. Iain is fast asleep. I make the decision there and then to book a dinner for us at the Chelsea Hotel. That's when I plan to tell Iain how I am really feeling.

I have my hair washed and blow-dried at the Modern Hairdresser, in Hillbrow. The chap who does my hair is from London and is talkative and funny. I lived in London for two years while training to be a midwife, so I know the city well. Nigel tells me he trained in Vidal Sassoon's top hairdressing school. He recently opened up his own place here in Hillbrow, and business is going well. We have a lot in common and I enjoy this hour of chat and pampering.

Back at our flat, I dress up for the occasion in a skirt I've always felt good in, and which I know Iain likes. I'm feeling a bit more light-hearted by the time I'm made up and ready.

The whole atmosphere in the Chelsea is seductive and luxurious. The candelabrum on our table sparkles and the lights are low. The waiters are attentive without being intrusive, and we take our time choosing from the menu. After a glass of delicious South African wine, I'm feeling more relaxed and I give Iain a smile. I'm so relieved that he is on my side, and I tell him so. I broach the subject of my unhappiness.

'Do you think I haven't noticed, Mo?' Iain takes my hand and looks into my eyes. 'I'm right here for you. Remember our vows: for better or for worse. Whatever you want to do, stay on here or go back to Shetland, I'll support you.'

'It's this racist thing, Iain, this spectre of apartheid that we'll have to live with if we stay here. I'm not sure I can do it.'

'It's a ludicrous concept and a crazy ideology,' says Iain. 'But whether we live with it or get out of here, it'll still go on.'

For the next two hours, while rain lashes the street outside, and flashes of lightning occasionally disturb our conversation, we thrash out our future. In between mouthfuls of scrumptious food, and sips of wine, we debate back and forth.

In the end, we decide to give it a go. It's a compromise, I suppose. We'll give our lives and our jobs all we've got for the next month. We'll try our best. After the month is up, we'll have another dinner at the Chelsea, talk over our thoughts and feelings, and come up with a final decision.

I've been dreading Monday, but here it is and I'm on my way along Empire Road to Noordgesig. Last night, the Highveld storm kept me awake, but it has undoubtedly washed the city clean. I just wish my head and my heart felt as fresh.

Half-heartedly, I park my car in the shade of the now-familiar old tree, and make my way to my office.

Singing, I hear singing. Who can it be?

The nursing staff is in the office, ready to fill me in and give me a report. But first, they raise their voices in unison. 'Welcome back, welcome back.'

I swallow hard and tears build up behind my eyes. 'Oh, thank you, thank you,' I manage to murmur. 'You are all so very kind.'

Then it's down to work. The clinic is already filling up. I listen carefully as Sister Rosie gives me a detailed report. I am shocked to learn that baby Craig Abrams, the baby we sent to Coronation Hospital before going on leave, died from his meningitis.

Sister Rosie and I agree that we will visit the Abrams family this afternoon. I have a word with Dr Sol about the case. We both hope that, one day soon, there'll be a vaccine to prevent this disease. Because of my personal experience of meningitis, I can identify, and empathise with their situation.

***

Judy Abrams welcomes Rosie and me into their tiny home. Despite the cramped conditions, it is sparkling clean. Water is supplied through a cold-water tap, and heated on the stove. I make a vow to myself that I'll never again complain about my Hillbrow flat.

We settle down for a cup of tea and Judy becomes tearful as she relates the story. 'He never woke up properly, just lay there moaning. He had a purple rash all over his body. The doctors were very kind and gave him an injection, but it was no use and he died.'

'I'm so sorry to hear this, Judy.' I tell her of my baby sister's death. I give her a hug and tell her she must keep in touch with us. 'Do you think you'll try for another baby?'

'Oh yes, we will. Tony and I have discussed this already and, once we feel it's time, we will try. Thank you for your concern, you and Sister Rosie will be the first to know if I'm successful.' When we say goodbye, she manages a tentative smile.

On our way back to the clinic along the dusty road, Sister Rosie says, 'Time for home. It's been quite a day and tomorrow will be much of the same, I should think. It will be a good idea for you to spend some time with Sidley. He'll explain how the administration works. I'll set up a meeting tomorrow, shall I?'

***

Book-keeping and accountancy, I tell Sidley in his cramped admin office, were never my strong subjects in school. "But I promise, I'll try my best to concentrate, and I do want to learn, so be patient with me."

He flashes me a wide, crooked smile, and I decide I like this young man.

'Well at least you're honest.' Sidley chuckles. 'As for me, I find accountancy fascinating. Getting it, all tallied up makes my day.'

'Are you an Accountant then?'

A fleeting sadness crosses Sidley's face. 'No, unfortunately, my mom died when I was still in school. My granny brought me and my sister up so, as soon as I could, I left school to look after them.'

After a couple of 'accountancy hours', I've had enough and am starting to get thirsty and a little bit bored. Sidley, on the other hand, is on a roll. He's telling me all about what his work involves, and how he and his colleagues work together as a team.

'All I can say, Sidley, is that I feel comfortable leaving all this in your hands. But enough of that for now, I'm boggled. I'd love to hear more about your family and the people of Noordgesig.'

I make us both a coffee and settle down to quiz him. Since he's a captive audience, and we've been getting on so well, I feel comfortable asking him more about apartheid. But, nonetheless, I make it clear that, if he feels he'd rather not talk about it, that's okay with me.

'It's fine by me, Sister McAlpine,' Sidley says, smiling broadly. I can tell he is highly amused by my questions, but I'm in deadly earnest. I need to know as much as I can if I'm to make my decision. This month will be over before we know it and I'm still wrangling with the problem in my head. There's so much I like about the country, and the work I'm doing here, but I can't get past the deep discomfort I feel over its policies.

Sidley fills me in knowledgably. 'The government is obsessed with colour. And, not only that, if we try to protest against the law, we can very quickly be arrested and thrown in jail.'

I have a flashback to my experience in Durban and give a shiver. Sidley notices and, misunderstanding, stands and closes the window.

'Many of the laws this government comes up with are ludicrous.' He drops back into his chair and takes a gulp of coffee. I mean, how crazy is it to try to classify human beings. And there's no scientific way to do it, of course, so the process is crass and crude.' His charming face has drawn into a scowl and lines of suffering show on either side of his mouth. 'Combs can be used to test how curly a person's hair is. Then there's the pencil test.'

'The pencil test?' I'm fascinated, but it's a horrified fascination.

Sidley crosses his leg and snorts. 'Oh yes. They stick a pencil in someone's hair. If the hair holds the pencil when they bend over, they're black. Just like that.'

Sidley and I sit in silence for a few minutes. Sidley's eyes are closed. Mine are wide open in shock. We're silent for a time, then Sidley opens his eyes and I catch sight of his irrepressible grin again.

'Anything else you want to know, I'm your man.'

'Well actually there is something bothering me.' Sidley gives me a quizzical look. 'I think Thomas doesn't like me.' I know I'm being blunt, but I carry on anyway. 'Maybe I'm being sensitive, but I definitely sense an undercurrent.'

Sidley looks concerned. 'It's not you, Sister. He keeps us all at arm's length. I think it's because he's having such a problem with his classification.'

'What do you mean? His ... racial classification?' It still sounds absurd on my tongue. 'But, why? I take it he's coloured, since he's working here in this clinic.'

'The thing is, Thomas's father is coloured and lives here

in Noordgesig, but his mother's black and lives in the next township of Orlando. Thomas's skin, as you can see, is very dark. Now, for some reason, the Race Reclassification Board wants to reclassify him as black.'

Suddenly everything makes sense, and I can understand the tragedy of his situation. I knew already that Thomas was born in Noordgesig and went to school here. It's my turn to close my eyes.

When I open them again, Sidley is standing at the window. He speaks without turning, so I can't see his face. 'I just hope he can stay coloured, otherwise he'll have to lose his job and move out of the area he's lived in all his life.'

My head is spinning while I try to process this information.

'Noordgesig is a bit of an anomaly, actually.' Sidley turns at last and returns to his chair. Although we're a coloured area, we're part of the greater township of Soweto. I honestly think the authorities didn't quite know what to do with this area at the tail end of Orlando, so they gave it to us.'

He gives a rueful chuckle. 'But I guess we're lucky to have a green area to look out on, and the river, of course.'

'I must say, I do love the view from my office window. It reminds me a little of my home in Scotland.'

'We might be distant relatives then,' says Sidley, perking up again. 'One of my ancestors was Scottish.'

Now that surprises me. 'Really, Sidley?'

He gulps at his coffee, leans back and nods. 'My granny has a big photograph hanging up in our living room. She's very proud of it. The man in the photo was her grandfather. He came out to South Africa during the Boer war, met and married my great grandmother … She, by the way, was as black as the ace of spades.'

He gives a great hoot of laughter. 'That will give you an idea of how many of the coloured people came about. My surname is Reid, a good Scots name.'

Then, just like that, I realise I'm laughing. It's a relief. I can feel the tension that I've been holding for too long ease a bit.

I leave Sidley in a much better frame of mind than I've been in for days. While our conversation didn't ease my concerns about apartheid, or how I might live comfortably within this system, it did entrench my sense of how special many of South Africa's people are. I feel a kinship with Thomas, with Sidley ... and his great-granddad, that intrepid Scot. If he could pave the way for me during those wild times, and find a place for himself, perhaps I might also find a role here, and a way to do some good.

***

A smiling Sister Hilda pokes her head into my office. 'The antenatal clinic is well underway, Sister McAlpine. Sister Maria suggests that you might like to come for a look.'

Eight pregnant mothers are waiting their turn when I join the midwives. I'm back in control today and the next three hours fly by, with me doing something that I love. I pitch in, helping to check the moms, and listening carefully to concerns from both moms and staff.

A pretty young woman called Dorothy tells me this will be her last visit. 'Oh really? But, you're only four months. Are you moving away?'

'Yes, I am. Not really what I want to do, but it's what I must do.'

I'm not concerned. People move all the time. I give her a smile. 'I hope you'll be happy. You'll get your maternity notes, and you'll check in with the midwives at the new clinic?'

There's a look of concern on Dorothy's face. 'I'm going to Swaziland.' Her big brown eyes are filling up with tears.

I do a quick mental check. Swaziland. Now, where exactly is Swaziland? A memory comes back from my school days: Basutoland, Botswana, Swaziland. But I can't quite remember where these countries sit in relation to South Africa.

'Why are you sad, Dorothy?'

Then the story pours out. Dorothy's boyfriend, the father of her baby, is a German immigrant. 'He loves me very much, Sister, and he sneaks out to our house when he can. But we think the police are onto us.'

Dorothy is weeping. I give her a handful of tissues and put my hand on her shoulder. In between sobs, she manages to tell me: 'Last week, he went to Swaziland and he's got a good job there. Now I'm going. My parents are devastated, but they're happy he's going to look after our baby and me.'

'Oh Dorothy, I'm so very sorry to hear this. Please do let us know, if you can, how you get on.'

'Thank you, I will. I'm sorry, I've made such a fool of myself.'

I give her arm a reassuring squeeze. 'Never, ever, Dorothy. You're very brave. I know you'll miss your parents. I know what that feels like, believe me. But I'm so pleased you have a good man to take care of you.' I raise my eyebrows and smile encouragingly and I'm rewarded with a small tentative smile back.

CHAPTER SEVEN

Getting stuck in

January 1970

'So how was your first day back?' Iain is all smiles. He's offered to make supper and he's chopping onions, while I pour us both a glass of wine.

'Thanks, darling, for giving me a break from the cooking. I'm exhausted. Yes, I've had a good day.'

Actually, it's been more like the curate's egg but, in the car on the way home, I decided to keep my inner turmoil to myself. I still feel out of my depth, but we decided to give it a month. No point in worrying him at this stage.

'I can see you're very tired,' Iain gives me a sympathetic look. 'Let's make it an early night.'

Not for the first time, I snuggle up against that work-hardened chest and say a silent prayer of thanksgiving for all the love and support that I need for now.

Tomorrow is another day. And the month isn't over yet.

***

I'm settling down and, as the days go by, I find that I'm enjoying my work. I make a point of chatting to the staff, one on one, and this is working well. I've always had a great interest in people and, once they see I'm genuinely concerned, they open up, and tell me their stories.

Sister Rosie laughs when I raise my concerns about Dorothy and what will become of her.

'*Moenie* worry *nie*,' she reassures me. I'm getting better at this language, I tell myself. 'This sort of thing happens all the time. Many of our young girls work in Jo'burg and there they meet white guys. Some do fall pregnant and some form loving relationships, which can cause problems with the authorities. But you know as well as I do...' That rather dour face lights up. She spreads her arms wide and a big, beautiful smile lifts her mouth. '...love always finds a way.'

'Ah Rosie, so true, you old romantic, you. So, she won't be reported to the police or arrested?'

'I doubt it, not before she's safely out of the country. We, as a community, have little recourse against the government, so we stick together and keep our mouths shut. Unless of course there is a blatant contravention of the law. Murder maybe?' Sister Rosie gives me a big wink.

***

As the days and weeks go by, I create a routine for myself. Up early, then off to work. There's plenty to do to take up my time. I love helping Dr Sol in the GP clinic. Then there's the family planning clinic, the well-baby clinic, the antenatal and postnatal clinics, not to mention the boring admin, but of course that has to be done too. By 4.30pm, I'm back in my car and off home.

Some days, I go out with the midwives to a home delivery, and that is what I enjoy the most. Back in the UK, childbirth is becoming more and more medicalised, so it's refreshing to go out and deliver babies in the way that Mother Nature intended.

Today turns out to be a special day. I help Sister Maria

deliver a breech baby. I arrive at the clinic as usual at 8.30am to hear that Maria is already out at a delivery.

'She's been out most of the night,' Sister Rosie informs me. 'It's Cathy Meyer, breech mommy. If you'd like to go, I know Sister Maria would appreciate an extra pair of hands.'

'I'd love that.'

It's not far away, so I hurry there on foot. I pass a group of schoolchildren along the way, and am heartened to see they are neatly dressed in faded uniforms.

'*Goeie môre*, Suster,' they call out, I call back, repeating their greeting, feeling proud of myself for trying out this new language.

I knock on the door of number 28 and am immediately greeted by a middle-aged woman holding a toddler in her arms. A young boy holds tight to her apron.

'Oh, so you're the new English Sister in charge of the clinic.' She introduces herself as Fanny Niehaus, smiles and holds out her hand. I take her work-hardened one in mine and confirm that I am indeed Sister McAlpine.

'Sister Maria is going to be happy to see you. We're all exhausted; it's been some night of it. Come on through and see Cathy.'

I'm led through the house. The linoleum floor is scuffed and chipped, and covered by a threadbare rug that must once have been red. But, as I've noticed in many of these homes, the poverty of the people doesn't prevent them from keeping the floors and surfaces as clean as possible.

Both the little ones are tearful and fractious, and the toddler has a trail of snot from nose to mouth so, once I've been introduced to Cathy, Fanny disappears with both children in tow.

Cathy Meyer is sitting upright on a small single bed, holding her abdomen. Her moans fill the room. Even so, she looks at me and says a quick hello before catching her breath.

'So good to see you here, Sister McAlpine.' A tired-looking Maria greets me warmly. I'm surprised at how calm and cool she is. If this were me, out all night at a breech delivery, I'd be hot, exhausted and altogether flustered.

'I've just examined her and I think she's almost ready. The last few contractions are getting stronger and closer together. She wants to push.' Maria is looking at me and her voice rises to be heard above Cathy's moans. 'I'm happy to let you deliver the baby.
you know the old saying of course, hands off the breech.' I nod and she goes on. 'What do you say?'

I swallow hard, and tell myself that this is my ideal time to learn. I've seen vaginal breech deliveries but, more and more these days, breech babies in the UK are delivered by caesarean section.

'I'd love to, but only if you supervise me. I've never delivered a breech so, if you're willing to take me on, I'll give it a go,'

'Good news,' Maria says, with a reassuring smile at Cathy. 'I've delivered plenty.' And to me: 'There's a clean gown and a pair of disposable gloves in my bag, help yourself.'

While I get myself gowned and gloved, Maria turns to Cathy. 'You're doing an excellent job. You must try very hard not to push at first. Breathe deeply, my dear, and try hard to relax, but not to push.' She tells Cathy to lie on her back, with her buttocks over the end of the bed. 'Use your hands to push your inner thighs apart. That will give baby more room to exit. Now, Sister McAlpine is going to kneel on the floor and she'll catch your baby.'

Cathy's perineum distends. I encourage her to keep

pushing her legs apart, and I see the baby's buttocks clearly. I listen in to foetal heart, and relieved to hear the beat loud and clear.

I know my voice is a bit shaky, but I carry on. 'Now, don't push, Cathy. Good girl, you're a champ. I want your baby to come slowly. The slower the better.'

Cathy is now grunting. Sister Maria's voice rings out. 'Don't push, Cathy, whatever you do, don't push.'

The baby's legs slide out easily. It's a little girl

Another contraction comes and, with it, the baby's body slides out as far as the shoulders.

Sister Maria hands me a warm towel and I wrap it firmly around baby's body. Most of her body is now exposed, and I must not allow her to get cold. Even in the hot South African climate I must take every precaution. If the shock of cold air makes her gasp, she will inhale amniotic fluid, which could be fatal. Secondly, the baby is slippery and the towel will give me something to grip on to if I need to manipulate her shoulders and head.

With the next contraction, the left shoulder is on its way out. Maria's voice commands: 'That's it, shoulder out, now rotate her body a little bit clockwise, yes good, again use your finger … and there's the right shoulder. Both her arms are out, Cathy, my dear. You really are doing very well.'

Cathy responds with a sigh and a grunt. Only the head now remains inside.

'Now, Cathy,' Maria intones, 'with the next contraction I want you to push with all your strength. We want her head out now.'

It takes another ten minutes before baby's head is almost out. Sister Maria hands me a swab, and I wipe baby's mouth and nose. A gasp and a cry are like music to my ears when I lift baby Meyer upside down by her ankles, then up and over onto Cathy's abdomen. Maria hands me the mucous catheter and I insert this gently into baby's mouth and suck on the other end to clear away fluid and mucous. Then I clear each nostril in the same way. Baby gasps, coughs, and lets out a lusty scream, and the blue tinge of her skin quickly changes to a healthy pink.

'Isn't that just the best noise?' says cool, calm Sister Maria. I silently nod, conscious that I'm shaking a bit, while I clamp and cut the cord. I wrap baby in a dry, warm towel then hand the precious bundle back to Cathy.

'Oh, she's so beautiful, so lovely,' exclaims Cathy. 'She's worth all the pain in the whole world.' It never fails to amaze me how quickly a mom forgets the pain of labour the moment she holds her new-born in her arms.

I've been so focused on the delivery that I've been unaware of my surroundings. I glance around now. The bedroom is sparse, the curtains faded, and I can't help wondering how Cathy will manage, bringing three under-five children up in this tiny house.

I hear Maria before I see her. She's laughing as she brings Ouma Fanny and the two little ones into the bedroom. She lifts both children up onto the bed and they snuggle up to their mommy. Fanny is giving what sounds like orders, while Maria shows the new baby off to her siblings.

Half an hour later, things have settled down in the Meyer house. Cathy's placenta is delivered and although her perineum is looking a bit bruised it's thankfully still intact, 'We'll keep an eye on the bleeding' says Maria. Dad Neville, I'm told, will be home around six o'clock. 'I can't wait to show baby Tina off,' Cathy says. 'He just loves kids.'

'Thank you for all your help, Sister McAlpine.' Maria is looking tired but unruffled. 'Why don't you get back to the clinic. I know you must be hungry and thirsty. I'm going to stay here for a bit with Cathy, I'll make sure all is OK. I'll bath baby Tina and weigh her, then I'm going home for a sleep. We can catch up with things tomorrow.'

It feels like an anti-climax. Adrenaline still pumps through my body. I would have loved a good old post-delivery chat with Maria, but I get the feeling that once I'm out of the way, she and the household will relax and laugh and let their hair down.

Back in the clinic, I meet Sister Rosie in the kitchen. 'Oh, you're back, how about a cup of tea? And more importantly, how was it?'

'I think it best if you ask Maria that question. I feel as if I've performed a miracle. Mom and baby are both doing well, and I thoroughly enjoyed the whole experience. Sister Maria is certainly a good midwife. I'm dying for that cup of tea and then I'm off home.'

Rosie lifts the teapot and looks at me searchingly. 'I understand. We'll drink to that and then we'll catch up tomorrow,'

CHAPTER EIGHT

Hard decisions and good news

April 1970

Iain is staring at me intently. 'So, what have you decided? Will we stay here...' He reaches across the table for my hand. '...or is it back to Shetland for us?'

We're in the Chelsea hotel – same ambiance, same low lighting, same feeling of luxury. Gosh! It seems no time at all since we were last here. Can it really be a month?

Iain squeezes my hand. 'You go first.' I detect concern in his voice.

The waiter hands me a menu, but I wave him away. 'Please give us another ten minutes.'

'Take your time Madam, Sir.' He gives us a reassuring smile, then retreats and makes his way to greet a couple coming in through the main door.

'I love my job, Iain. It's exciting and not a day goes by without my learning something. The staff are great.' I search through my handbag for a clean tissue, blow my nose, and then take a mouthful of water.

'There's a but coming, isn't there?' he asks quietly. I nod.

'It's this strange apartheid thing that gets me. I often think to myself that it would have been easier if I'd been sent to a black clinic, more straightforward ... Sorry, I'm maybe not making myself clear. All I can say is, then black would be black, and white would be white.'

I shrug my shoulders, let out a big sigh and go on. 'But this coloured clinic, or mixed-race clinic, sure gets me mixed up.'

Iain keeps quiet, watching me closely, then nods and smiles at my word-play, while I continue to give voice to my confused thoughts.

I tell him about the pencil test and the classification law. Even to my own ears, the story I'm telling sounds as if I'm making it up.

An incredulous look flits across Iain's face. 'If this story wasn't coming out of your mouth, Mo, I wouldn't believe it. Well, I suppose that's it then. Back to Shetland it is?'

'I'm not going to let you off.' I keep my face deadpan but, inside, I feel so blessed to have a man who would do anything for me. 'Come now, let me hear your thoughts about South Africa.'

'I really do like it here. Love is maybe too strong a word, but I do love so much about it. The sunshine, for starters. I'm told this is the best climate in the world.' A big, sunny smile crosses Iain's face. 'Being readily accepted into the music world is another plus and I do love my job and my workmates. I could go on and on, Mo but, what I'm saying is neither here nor there. If you're unhappy, then I'm unhappy.'

It's my turn now to take Iain's hand. In fact, I take both his hands. 'Well, that's so good to hear, because I'm staying.'

'What are you saying?' There's a big crease now between Iain's eyebrows. 'Sometimes, Mo, with you I'm at a loss for words.'

'The thing is, I'm pregnant, my darling.'

***

Pregnancy suits me and, as my tummy grows, so does my confidence. The clinic staff are happy for me. They mother and nurture me and I enjoy it. 'You're so kind and understanding to us, so let us do something nice for you.' I hear this over and over during the weeks and months that follow.

I throw myself into my work. I particularly enjoy my well-baby clinics. What I see there is a far cry from my previous experiences in clinics in the UK where, thanks to the National Health Service, malnutrition and the worst effects of grinding poverty are seldom encountered. Not so here in the townships of South Africa.

Noordgesig has its fair share of problems but, because it's a relatively small township compared with the larger ones throughout Soweto, our two health visitors work hard at monitoring potential hazards like neglect and abuse. If and when concerns do arise, we have a meeting, and then decide if we should refer the case to the social welfare department. We offer two baby and child health clinics every week, where we promote healthy eating and encourage breastfeeding.

The family planning clinic can be fun. I love teaching health education, and I like to think I have some success in persuading women that planning their babies is the sensible option. Most women are happy with this, while others are not shy in expressing their opinion that this is yet another apartheid scheme to cut down on the black population.

The young moms generally have a great sense of humour and much risqué talk is enjoyed among them. The health department sends us boxes of condoms free of charge but, quite honestly, they're a waste of time because the latex is so thick. A far cry from Durex, methinks.

'*Ag, Suster*, my man hates these things at the best of times, but this big lump that you're offering me is more suited to a horse.' This is followed by guffaws and nods and light-hearted banter.

Sol is a busy doctor, and I enjoy sitting in as his nurse. Tuberculosis is an ongoing problem in South Africa. Many of the patients we see suffer from Pulmonary TB, the most common type and, after they've been diagnosed, and sometimes hospitalised, these patients will continue to attend our clinic.

One of our patients is Tom, a regular visitor to the clinic. One bright Tuesday, it occurs to me that, unless time is flying by at an alarming rate, I saw him not so very long ago. I take a look at his case notes and see he should have medication dispensed monthly. Not every Tuesday morning! It strikes me that his clinic visits have become a little *too* regular. I decide to have a chat with him.

'You're looking well, Tom.' He nods and smiles back at me. 'I'm sure it's the good medicine you're on. I see you only need to come once every month, but I've noticed you're here at the dispensary every week.'

'Ag Sister, I lose them and misplace them and then I just forget.'

'Maybe you should come and see Doctor Sol about your forgetfulness?'

'I don't need Dr Sol.' Tom stands up to his full height of over six feet. 'I'm an *Inyanga*, you see.'

'*Inyanga*, Tom? I'm sorry, I don't understand.' Actually, I do understand. An *Inyanga* is a traditional healer, specialising in herbal medicine. But I want him to spell it out.

Tom's face lights up, and he takes great pride in

explaining what a good doctor he is. 'Lots of sick people come and see me and I give them good medicine.'

Ah ha, maybe I'm onto something. But I have to be careful what I say. 'My goodness me, Tom, you're a doctor. So why do you come to us if you can treat yourself?'

'I mix your *muti* into my *muti*.' I already know that, in many parts of Africa, medicine is called *muti*.

'Oh, I see, Tom. By the way, do you treat many patients?'

'Yes, I do, I'm a very good Inyanga, lots of folk come to me,' Tom grins at me. He's a handsome fellow, with his square white teeth, and he has a charming manner. I'm betting that he has indeed got lots of clients.

'I'll tell you what,' I say, giving Tom a broad smile, 'I'll speak with Dr Sol, and he'll give you a letter to take with you to Coronation Hospital. He'll request that you have a check-up and an X-ray. Meantime, the dispensary will give you your *muti*, but that will be the last time, until we hear back from Coro.'

Sol and I have a chat about my suspicions. 'Well, it's a dangerous practice if what you suspect is true. As you know, messing around with the treatment can contribute to drug resistant TB. Not only is Tom putting himself at risk, but if he's mixing the medicine with his herbal *muti* —' Sol shakes his head and grimaces. 'No wonder drug resistant TB is becoming a big problem. I'll have a word with the Coronation specialist.'

At first, we wait for Tom's return, wondering how he'll react to having had his drug supply cut off. When he still hasn't turned up some time later, we begin to worry about his welfare. Our clinic staff put out feelers and tell us the word on the street is that he left for Cape Town – perhaps to seek out another well-meaning but more gullible clinic sister.

The weeks and months pass all too quickly. More and more, I'm enjoying working in the clinic, and I'm also enjoying being pregnant. I'm feeling settled and Iain is happy. He does worry about me being in the townships, but I constantly reassure him that I feel completely safe there.

CHAPTER NINE
All manner of creepie-crawlies

I'm writing reports when I hear shouts and laughter outside my office window. I look up. Five young men are making their way in the direction of the stream that runs past the clinic. I can't see the stream from my window, though, since it's hidden by a high embankment. I don't pay much attention, but I do notice one of the men is carrying a large empty beer bottle.

It's the end of my working day when I notice a large cloud of smoke emerging from the direction of the stream. Sol has already gone and I'm getting my things together. Next thing, I hear whooping and shouting, and five heads appear over the embankment. One chap is stark naked from his waist down. He's screaming and holding fast to his genitals.

I start to become concerned when I see they're running towards the clinic. I call two of the nurses, Greta and Miriam. By this time, the five men are inside the clinic, where they continue to shout and laugh. What a racket. The smell of marijuana is strong and it makes me cough.

The half-naked guy is in great distress and tears run down his face. '*Sny hom af, sny hom af,*' he shouts, '*asseblief,*

Suster.' When he sees me, he calms down a little, although his eyes still plead with me. I understand enough Afrikaans by now to know that he is asking me to cut 'it' off.

I realise that I have to take charge of the situation before it gets out of hand. I point to three of the men. 'Greta, please take these three out to the waiting room. Miriam, please take these two into the treatment room.'

I look directly at my patient and his friend. 'I'm sorry that I don't understand Afrikaans very well, so please tell Nurse Miriam what's wrong and why you're here but, first of all, I'll need to know your names.'

'My name is Terry,' the unafflicted young man says. He points a finger at his poor bedraggled friend, still clutching his penis. 'He's Lionel.'

Lionel reminds me of an innocent little boy. He's confused and baffled and sobbing. I try to be gentle with him, until at last he allows me to take his arm and help him up onto the bed. The thought runs through my head that he's probably preparing himself for me to actually cut 'it' off. I examine his problem genitals, while his eyes search mine beseechingly. 'Sorry Sister, I'm sorry.'

I'm pleased to see that Terry and Miriam are in conversation. Then Miriam calls out, 'It was a spider, Sister McAlpine. Lionel was bitten by a spider.'

Thank goodness for that clear diagnosis. I examine Lionel and, sure enough, I can see the bite on his red, swollen scrotum.

'Now Lionel, listen carefully to me.' I take his hand and bend my head so that we are face to face. 'You are going to be just fine, and I'm certainly not going to cut it off.'

I'm praying that my voice and smile are convincing enough. 'Maybe you'll make lots of babies one of these days.'

Miriam gives a little giggle, then exclaims, 'Sister is

so right, Lionel.' We're rewarded with a very small smile. A tetanus jab, an antibiotic and a strong pain killer, along with a comforting dressing, are duly administered. I smile reassuringly at Lionel and tell him that I'll see him tomorrow. This time, I'm happy to see a bigger, more confident smile. Then I'm off home, leaving the nurses to deal with the aftermath.

Next morning, before I write up the medical notes, I call Miriam and Greta to hear the story of Lionel and the spider.

The two nurses tell me that smoking dagga is common among the coloured men. It's illegal, but apparently easy to come by. The neck of a beer bottle is cut off from the body of the bottle, and filled with dagga – the local name for marijuana – which then acts like a rudimentary pipe. Dagga, smoked enthusiastically like this, creates great clouds of smoke. So, that accounts for the billows of smoke I saw yesterday emanating from the bank of the stream.

The dagga party was interrupted when Lionel let out his piercing scream and ripped his pants and underwear off. The others couldn't help laughing when they saw a spider crawl out from between Lionel's legs.

'People believe that the poison from the bite can get into the bloodstream and kill the person,' Greta tells me. 'That's why Lionel was shouting for you to cut it off.'

I tell Miriam and Greta how impressed I am with them. We have a good chuckle before settling down and analysing the situation, considering what we did right, and if there was anything we could have done better. We end up writing a full report and both nurses agree to do a home visit with me, to confirm that Lionel is recovering.

He lives with his girlfriend, his sister and her husband, who are parents to three school-going children. The house is overcrowded and dirty, not unusual, apparently, in

Noordgesig. I take note of this and will record it on Lionel's case notes but, alas, I'm thinking, there isn't much I can do about it

'How are you, Lionel? I'm glad to see you're up and about.' I give him a bright smile.

'It's very sore,' he says, not meeting my eyes, 'but the pain tablets are helping.'

I tell Lionel I'll need to examine his injury and that Miriam and Greta will also have to see what's going on. I'm relieved the swelling is subsiding.

I leave the nurses to attend to the dressing before turning back to Lionel, 'You're doing fine, but you'll need to come to the clinic every day until we're happy.'

We take our leave with Lionel looking decidedly sheepish, and repeating how sorry he is.

***

Abel, our handyman and cleaner, is a great favourite of mine. Every morning, he greets me with, 'How are you, Sister and how is the baby?'

He's taken it upon himself to protect me from the snakes and the spiders that lurk around the clinic. For sure, there are plenty of spiders but, thank goodness, I've yet to see a snake. The other scourge he protects me from is cockroaches, in their hundreds.

Many a morning I find him in my office with his tin of paraffin and a rag but, nonetheless, I've had to grow used to the 'whoosh' of the cockroaches as I open the drawer in my rickety old desk. Abel does his best to exterminate these horrible pests, but they always come back. I'm hoping that my application for a new desk will come through but, until such time, I'll depend on Abel and his paraffin.

CHAPTER TEN
Protest and disquiet

October 1970

A memo comes through, requesting that I attend a meeting in Orlando Clinic. Not giving this much thought, I join my charge sister colleagues, to be told that the health department has decided to offer a polio vaccination programme to all children in Soweto.

It's a simple exercise, during which we drive vans through the townships, using loudhailers to call on parents to bring their children for a sugar-lump vaccine.

All goes well and it's fun too until, in the second week of the exercise, we are abruptly told that we will have to discontinue the programme, because rumours are circulating that this is a government ploy to poison the children.

I'm feeling uneasy when I relate the story to the clinic staff. I note that Thomas is staring at me in a decidedly unfriendly manner. I've heard no more about his reclassification, but I'm glad he's still with us. I don't blame him for disliking me. I would feel the same, I'm sure, if I were walking in his shoes.

'There's a lot of unrest in the townships,' says Sister Rosie over morning coffee.

Part of my remit is to train whoever I think would be a

good candidate for taking charge of and managing a clinic. There is a push for 'Africanising' the Soweto clinics. Sister Rosie is my choice.

She walks over to the window and looks out in silence for a couple of minutes. I keep quiet. She clears her throat, then carries on.

'"Worried" might be too strong a word, but I'm definitely concerned about your safety here in Soweto. Our people are getting edgy and dissatisfied with their lives under the yoke of apartheid.' She comes over to my chair and puts a motherly arm around my shoulders. To say I'm touched is an understatement. I feel a lump rising in my throat.

'Oh, my dear, I do thank you for your concern, but I don't understand. What do you think might happen to me?'

'There's an undercurrent of dissatisfaction and anger here in Soweto all the time, it's nothing new.' Rosie is clearly upset. She lifts her shoulders, lets out a sigh and smiles ruefully, 'I'm sure it's been here since 1948 when the Afrikaans government came to power. But getting back to your question: you saw what happened with the vaccine. It will take very little to get a riot going, and I'd hate for you to be caught up in it.'

'I'll be leaving to have my baby,' I say. 'Then who knows what will happen. By the way, Sister Rosie, I'm so pleased with your work and your knowledge too. If I decide not to come back...' It's my turn now to put an arm around her shoulder. '...nothing would please me more than for you to take over my job.'

Another two weeks go past. I'm looking forward now to having a break, and excited at the prospect of my baby arriving.

***

November 1970

It's Sol's half day, and time for me to pack up and go home. I'm looking forward to eating out tonight with friends. I'm humming to myself and considering what I'll wear. I get into my car and drive on to the road and, to my dismay, I see a crowd, no, a mob, of people on the road, blocking my way.

'Oh God, help me,' I say out loud. They're carrying stones and it seems to me they have raging anger and hatred in their eyes. The mob surges forward and they're headed straight for me.

Time seems to slow as my pulse races and I can feel the adrenaline pumping through my body. I have a vision of my baby and I pray that this adrenaline rush will not affect my unborn. Then I go on instinct. I put my foot down hard on the accelerator, close my eyes and go for it. To stop the car would be fatal, or so I'm thinking. The car revs and shoots off. I'm waiting to feel a body under the wheels. That doesn't happen, but what I can hear is the back window smashing and thuds on the doors of the car.

I keep driving and, all the time, I'm telling myself to calm down, calm down. I'm shaking like a leaf. I dare not look back. I see Coronation Hospital up ahead. Good, I'm on my way.

My heart is racing as I navigate my way home. I pull into the parking bay, bite my lips hard to stop myself from giving in to my emotions. Time for that when I'm in Iain's embrace.

I gingerly step out of the car and stand up on shaky legs. I feel my tummy and am reassured that all is well. I feel a kick, but no contraction. I'm thankful there's no one around to ask awkward questions.

I am so hoping Iain is at home, but no such luck. I stumble to our bed and let the tears flow.

I'm a crumpled mess when Iain finds me. He takes me in his arms. 'When you're ready to talk, I'm here. I see the car is a wreck, but that's neither here nor there. I'm so thankful you're in one piece.'

Through crying, hiccoughing, and more crying, I finally manage to tell Iain what happened. I take my time going over the incident. Iain is sympathetic and understanding. I know my husband well, and I can tell that, beneath the soft demeanour is a very real anger. 'First, let's get you into a warm bath and then we'll take it from there.'

What a relief it is to be able to share my worries and my fears.

'Don't even think about going back to Soweto,' Iain says, after listening to the evening news on the radio. 'That's a no-go area.'

By now I'm feeling better and am able to think straight. Iain takes charge. 'I'm going to take over now, Mo. Tomorrow, first thing, I'll ring Miss Clark. In any case, you're due to leave by the end of this month. Next, I'm going to make an appointment with the midwives. I'll insist they see you tomorrow, just to make sure everything's in order. I'm due holidays, so I'm going to take some time off to be on hand to look after you.'

I surprise myself by sleeping soundly and wake up to find Iain and our midwife in our bedroom. After a thorough consultation, midwife Jane tells me with a big smile that she's happy with baby and, from now on, I must rest and relax.

I am sad to leave the clinic staff so abruptly, but I'm also deeply relieved to be out of there in this climate. I keep contact with my colleagues for some years but, sadly, never do discover what happened to Thomas, and his pending reclassification.

True to his promise, Iain has booked us into a luxurious health spa for a long weekend of pampering and relaxation. By the time I go into labour, a week early, I'm well rested, and my joy is complete when my beautiful baby boy Iain Callum is placed in my arms.

The next years of my life are spent with my family. A joyous time, especially when my second son Erlin Sven is born in January 1975. I am fortunate to have Iain's mother Leila come and stay with us in Johannesburg to help me bring up our boys.

CHAPTER ELEVEN

Uprising on a sunny winter's day

June 16, 1976 is a typical Johannesburg highveld winter's day, cold and sunny with a sparkling blue sky. I'm off to the park with Erlin-Sven cosy in his buggy. At a year and a half, he's all blond hair and rosy cheeks.

I'm loving being a Mum and housewife with Iain and my boys. Grace is on hand to help, since she came to work for us full-time.

Big brother Iain is by my side, proudly sporting Granny Leila's hand-knitted Fair Isle jumper that's come all the way from our home in the Shetland Isles.

'How many months now, Mummy, till I go to school?'

'Not long, just six months,' I reply, knowing too well that will sound like a life-time in a little boy's mind. We hadn't a care in the world, having just moved into our very first bought home. It cost Iain R15 000, an awful lot of money and, although we do sometimes wonder if we'll ever pay off the mortgage, this is the last thing on my mind this morning.

We reach the beautiful Rhodes Park, where I unpack our picnic lunch. Avocado sandwiches it is. I've finally acquired a taste for this deliciously exotic fruit, so plentiful in South Africa. The boys love them too and we are pleased to see that our new garden has a couple of Avo trees. Then it's fun on the jungle gym, swings and see-saws.

Back home and tired, the boys are more than ready for supper and their evening bath. I switch on the radio while preparing the evening meal. TV is only just making its appearance in South Africa – the government's thinking being that it would spread communism and immorality.

While I potter away in the kitchen – it's Wednesday, so I'm making spaghetti bolognaise – Iain and the boys are having a bubble-bath time, squealing and laughing.

'This is SABC Radio News at 7,' the newsreader begins in her usual dulcet tones. I don't pay too much attention, and then my ears prick up. 'Schoolchildren in Soweto are on the march in protest against school subjects being taught in the Afrikaans language.'

My stirring spoon hits the floor with a clatter. It's almost a relief, as I've been waiting for something like this for years. Am I surprised? No. Am I prepared? No.

It eventually comes to light that the SABC played down the full extent of the rioting and killings that took place, a mere 20km from where the news was being broadcast.

This is the picture we put together over the next few days, from newspaper reports and snippets of news we hear on the grapevine.

On that morning, thousands of students from the various townships within Soweto gather at their schools to participate in a student-organised demonstration. Many carry placards reading, 'Down with Afrikaans' and 'Down with Bantu Education'. Others sing freedom songs, as the unarmed crowd of schoolchildren marches towards Orlando soccer stadium where a peaceful rally has been planned.

The crowd swells to more than 10 000 students. About 50 policemen stop the students in an attempt to turn them back. At first, the police try unsuccessfully to disperse them with warning shots and teargas. Then security forces fire directly into the crowd of demonstrators. Many students retaliate by throwing stones.

The students carry on marching until they reach Orlando High School. A teargas cannister is lobbed by a white policeman into the front of the crowd. The crowd retreats slightly but remains facing the security police. Another policeman draws his revolver and a single shot is fired. There is a split second of silence. Then pandemonium breaks out. Children scream. More shots are fired. Students fall, while others run screaming from the carnage.

Sam Nzima, a news photographer, catches on camera the most defining photo of the struggle against apartheid. Thirteen-year-old Hector Pietersen is one of the first children to die, and becomes the image of the 1976 Soweto uprising. Nzima's photo shows Hector's body being carried by another student, Mbuyisa Makhubo, while his sister Antoinette runs beside them. It is published around the world.

Despite the fact that I witnessed the simmering discontent in the country first-hand, Iain and I are shocked when it finally boils over and we watch with great heartache as the state cracks down on a generation of young people who are merely trying to fight for what they are due – what we consider to be normal.

There is nothing much we can do, except to try to serve all the people of our adopted country the best way we know how and, from my point of view, to try to ease the suffering of those who need me.

CHAPTER TWELVE

The Marymount years

December 1978

I've been toying with the thought of going back to work. Iain junior is in school and Erlin-Sven will start nursery school next month. Granny Leila has been living with us for some time and is a great help with bringing up our boys. Between her and Grace, I'm beginning to feel that I'm on one long holiday.

Thinking about holidays, we have been on many. Iain has fitted our Kombi out with beds, a fridge and a comfortable tent. We truly are happy campers. We've been all over South Africa, from the Kruger Park to Cape Town, travelled the Garden Route and seen the spectacular mountains and gorges of the Eastern Transvaal.

I'm enjoying life as a housewife and mother, but my calling to return to midwifery and nursing is giving me itchy feet. My good friend Flo McKenzie, who hails from Aberdeen, is a fellow Scot and a midwife. She persuades me to join her at her place of work, the Marymount Maternity Hospital in Kensington. Flo and I are like sisters and have supported each other through our years in South Africa, since meeting at St Marks Presbyterian church.

The Marymount is a Roman Catholic hospital, established in 1949 by the Dominican order of nuns, and is conveniently within walking distance of our house. It is ideal for work and would allow me to be near my family.

The office of Sister Kieran, Matron of the Marymount, looks out over a beautiful terraced garden, ablaze with exotic flowers and shrubs. Coming from the Shetland Islands, where the hills are covered in heather, and where trees are sadly lacking, I'm entranced.

Matron Kieran, a plump motherly nun, takes my hand and greets me with a smile. I can see teacups and biscuits on her desk. 'I thought we could have a chat over a cup of tea,' she says in her beautiful Irish brogue. I worked with, and made lifelong friends of many Irish nurses during my training years in the UK, so I immediately feel at home.

Two hours go past in a flash. Matron Kieran wants to know my nursing history, and is interested to learn that I've worked in the Soweto townships. 'We've plenty of black mothers delivering their babies here at the Marymount,' she says.

'Really, Sister? How does that work? How do you manage to get black and white folks mixing?'

'This hospital was built in 1949, just after the National Party came to power,' she says, pouring us both another cup of tea. 'There was a demand for a private maternity hospital here in Johannesburg, and that is how we came into being.' She lifts her shoulders, shakes her head and laughs. 'The church applied many caveats. We insisted, for instance, that we would admit black as well as white mothers. And the government accepted that condition.'

'They also made their own demands.' Another big smile. 'It finally ended up with the first floor being allocated to the black, coloured and Asian mums and the second floor allocated to the white mums. A compromise, I suppose.'

'Matron Kieran, I can see this is going to be an exciting challenge. Right up my street after working in the townships.'

***

March1979

My first day on duty on the second-floor postnatal ward, I'm given a tour by Charge Sister Natalie, a beautiful German nun whom everyone is in awe of, and many of the doctors are more than a little in love with.

'It's a busy floor, Sister McAlpine. We can have 50 moms here, plus their babies, at any one time.' She takes my arm and leads me into the main nursery. 'Our assistant nurses are Portuguese, and we train them in-house. They're bright and quick to learn.'

She explains that Mozambique and Angola both got independence recently, which was followed by an exodus of Portuguese people from both countries into South Africa, mainly Johannesburg.

'Many only just escaped with their lives, fleeing the civil war.' We approach a cluster of nurses busy changing nappies and cleaning the nursery.

'I'll leave you with the nurses, so that you can get to know them.' She introduces me to Nurse Maria, Rosa, Samara and Catia. I find them friendly and willing to chat. Maria and Catia have lived nearby in Kensington for years while Rosa and her sister Samara, originally from Mozambique, have an interesting tale to tell. I soon pick up on their life stories and how much they enjoy working at the Marymount.

Samara, the chatty one, has a strong Portuguese accent

and speaks English well. 'It is good to be here and to find employment. At first, we had to live in our car, me and Rosa and Mom and Dad.'

I'm taken aback by this. 'Really Nurse Samara?'

Samara's face is tense, 'We lived in a nice house in Lourenco Marques – my dad is an engineer. When the rebels came, we ran from the house, Dad grabbed his wallet and mom's purse, and led the way to the treehouse he'd built for us as children, high up in a tree at the back of our garden. We kept praying and, from where we were, watched the rebels ransack our home.'

Her voice cracks. I put my arm around her shoulders and tell her we can talk again another day, if it's too much for her now, but she's eager to finish her story.

'Fortunately, they didn't see our car, parked outside. We sat in the treehouse all night, until we were sure the coast was clear. Then we ran to the car and left with the clothes on our back. We knew no one here, so we parked up in Bez Park and stayed there for a month.'

Samara fastens her final nappy and returns the baby to its crib. She turns back to me. 'My mom heard about the Marymount from the lady who ran the shop where she bought our bread and milk. That's what we lived on for a month. Slowly things got better, Dad got a job and the Marymount took us in and found us a house.'

'You and your family are very brave,' I say, squeezing her hand in sympathy.'

'We are forever grateful to the Marymount sisters.'

I settle down easily at the Marymount. This is a happy time for me. Sister Natalie and I become firm friends. We are the same age and have much in common. As time goes on, she leaves me in charge of the ward. She has a true calling, and is happy to dedicate more of herself and her time to her vocation.

Each morning I do a ward round, spending personal time with the mothers. This can often take me until midday, but it's time well spent. I can answer their queries, address their complaints, and supervise the staff.

I get on well with the staff, both nursing and domestic. I keep my ears open and bring their complaints, when appropriate, to the notice of Sister Natalie or Matron Kieran.

The male cleaners have an on-going complaint regarding their uniforms. The tunic top is not a problem, it's the long shorts they hate. 'This is no good, Sister McAlpine,' says Simon with contempt in his voice. 'We feel like children. We want to wear jeans.'

I don't have much success with this complaint when I bring it to Matron Kieran. 'Sorry, Sister,' she says, 'not jeans. Rules from the top, unfortunately.'

The mothers come from all walks of life. Most employed people in South Africa have medical insurance of one kind or other. Some of the mothers are private fee-paying women who book the best rooms, while others come from middle- and working-class backgrounds and their fees are paid by their medical insurance. Once overheads are paid for, and this includes salaries, the profits from the Marymount go to Catholic mission hospitals throughout South Africa.

I come into frequent contact with women from a wide range of backgrounds: Portuguese, Greek, Italian, Jewish, Lebanese, as well as Afrikaans and UK immigrants. Then, of course, there are woman from the black, coloured and Asian communities. I love learning about their varied and diverse cultures and religious beliefs.

I know very little about the Roman Catholic faith. I'm

fascinated when the nuns tell me to pray to St Anthony if I lose something. 'He's the saint of lost things,' I'm told, and, 'St Jude is the saint of impossible causes.' Being brought up in the Protestant faith, I listen and observe with interest, and keep my thoughts to myself.

Then there are the Jewish mothers. Jewish baby boys are circumcised on the eighth day. If they are still in the Marymount at that time, we set up a room where the bris is performed by a rabbi or mohel. The bris is often followed by tea and goodies. We don't attend the ceremony but, when it's over, we often get to enjoy the left-over cake.

In the western world, childbirth is becoming more and more medicalised. The private sector in South Africa hasn't escaped this trend. Intervention before and during labour is all too common, and caesarean section delivery is becoming increasingly, and alarmingly, common. In my experience, many mothers would love to have had their babies without unnecessary intervention.

June 1983

After a couple of years of resistance, mainly from the doctors, who, after all, make their living from their private patients, I finally approach the management of the Marymount and also the senior nursing nuns, and put my idea of starting an active birth unit, which would allow the pregnant women to be in control of their birthing experience, supervised and looked after by midwives.

To my surprise and delight, I get the go-ahead. The unit is close to the labour ward so, if obstetric intervention becomes necessary, help is at hand.

The active birth unit is a success. We are inundated

with mothers who are keen to book the unit. Three rooms are converted into attractive private family rooms, complete with a comfortable double bed and bathroom. A birthing pool is installed, which proves to be a boon for easing pain and, if desired, mom can have an underwater birth.

One of the first expectant mothers to see the suite is a Mrs Anne Ferguson, who tells me: 'Both my babies were born in London. I'm thrilled you have this facility, it's just like the one I enjoyed back when Steven and Katie were born. This time I'd love to try for an underwater birth. What do you think, Sister?'

'I don't see why not, let's wait and see when the time comes.'

Anne Ferguson does have the birth she desires, and her husband Kevin participates in the whole event. Once baby Mia is safely delivered, he rushes home to collect the two older siblings. Their reaction to seeing mom, and being introduced to baby Mia, is a joy to behold.

CHAPTER THIRTEEN

The baby in the dustbin

September 1984

While the rest of the private hospitals and clinics throughout Johannesburg are installing and upgrading their premature baby nurseries and facilities, the Marymount is sadly lacking in neonatal intensive care.

Having an interest in premature babies, I offer to go to the Johannesburg General Hospital to train in neonatology, so that I can establish an intensive care baby unit in the Marymount.

Neonatology is a demanding course and takes up a lot of my time. I thoroughly enjoy it, and get lots of support from Iain and the family. After many months of hard work, I pass my exams. The hard work doesn't stop there, though. Since it's a specialist unit, employing the right staff is a challenge. Then we must install the ventilators and the open ICU incubators, the blood gas machine and the X-ray department.

We get through it all, though, and I finally set up Marymount's first NICU. I'm appointed charge sister, along with my other duties. More hard work, no doubt, but I'm delighted and Iain is very proud.

***

Four months pass.

It's 5.30am and I'm sound asleep when the call comes from the night sister. Sister Edith sounds frantic. 'There's a woman in the foyer with a baby in a plastic shopping bag and it's wrapped up in newspaper. She tells me she found it beside a dustbin in Jules Street. What must I do?'

I'm suddenly wide awake. 'I take it this baby is alive?'

'Yes, and it's whimpering. 'There's panic now in Edith's voice. 'It looks about 30-weeks' gestation.'

First things first, I'm thinking. Calm Edith down.

I reassure Sister Edith, and tell her to follow my instructions. 'Take the woman and the baby to a side room in the premature nursery. Until we know more, isolate baby in an incubator and, if need be, give oxygen, then phone the paediatrician. I'm on my way.'

The Marymount has funds put aside in a charity account specifically for situations like this, so I'm quite safe, from a financial view point, to admit this baby. ICU is not cheap and I surmise that this will cost a lot of money.

So be it, I tell myself.

Dr Kemp is a favourite doctor with all of us in the unit. He gives me a broad smile when I arrive. 'Except for prematurity, this little baby, surprisingly enough, considering she was found in the street, is doing fine.'

I've known Dr Kemp for ages and I know our new baby will be well-cared for. 'A strange story, I must say.' He lifts his eyebrows and looks at me expectantly. 'Are you positive you want to keep her here?'

'For the meantime, yes. I'll review the case with the nuns and the management and we'll come up with a plan. What do you say, Dr Kemp, are you willing to look after her? Before you say anything, I can reassure you that your fees will be paid.'

'Of course, I'll take her on. Her chest X-ray and oxygen levels are looking good. I'll leave the rest to you.'

In no time at all, we're all in love with baby Nandi. The nursing staff has come up with this lovely name and many of the parents who have babies in the unit love her too, and bring her toys and presents. She's a strong baby and, once the feeding tube is removed, she suckles well, starts to gain weight and thrives. Zanele, the woman who brought her to us, visits frequently and takes an interest in her progress.

I contact the welfare department, who are willing to transfer Nandi to Baragwanath Hospital. 'Once she is ready for discharge from Bara,' I'm told by Janelle, a rather abrupt social worker, 'she'll go to Orlando Orphanage.' Her voice softens. 'I'm sorry Sister, but that's the reality, she'll join the many children there.'

'Thank you, Janelle, I'll get back to you.'

***

I send the nursing staff to tea and am alone in the unit. I try to avoid the Nandi problem, but I know that, sooner or later, I'll have to face the inevitable. She's now out of the incubator and in a cot. I pick up her chart. She looks at me with inquisitive eyes and smiles. Sixty-nine days, I read. I put the chart down, and pick this little chocolate box baby up, and give her a big cuddle. 'No, it can't be,' I say out loud. 'You'll have to go, my darling.'

I take the chart to the phone, just inside the nursery door. I pick up the receiver, and look out through the picture window. A black woman with a toddler strapped to her back is hurrying towards the nursery. I replace the receiver. I'll first see what she needs, then I'll face this difficult task again.

'Can I help you?' I ask, when she reaches me.

She nods. 'Please.'

I take her to my office, where I learn her name is Nellie. Nellie's face is covered in sweat. She cradles the toddler on her lap and sits unmoving.

I take two deep breaths and instruct myself to relax. Intuition tells me this isn't going to be an easy conversation. Whatever she wants, I can see it's taken a lot for her to come here. I paste a smile on my face and sit down across from her.

'What's your little boy's name, Nellie, and how old is he?'

'Lucas, fourteen months.'

'I can see you're very hot. Would you like a glass of water or a cup of tea, maybe?'

Her trembling hand relaxes when she reaches for the water. I reckon she's in her mid- thirties. She's wearing a house maid's overall and strong shoes.

I sit back down, cross my legs and feel my own hands clench. 'Now Nellie, tell me why you're here.' I try to smile encouragingly.

'My baby is here.'

The story comes out in bits and pieces. Nellie is employed as a housemaid not far from the Marymount. She has five children, four of whom live with her mother in Soweto. Lucas lives with Nellie.

'My madam is a very nice woman but she told me after I had Lucas that, if I kept on having babies, I would have to go. I asked Zanele to help me get rid of the baby. We used sticks and a wire, but when the baby came out it was alive. It was alive, it was alive.' She keeps repeating the words, like a mantra. Tears are now gushing from her eyes.

Lucas, clinging to his mom, is adding his protests.

'Mama, Mama.'

I briefly leave Nellie and call Sister Thembi to come and give me a hand. Then I leave them alone while I catch my breath, and go for a break. I've seen illegal abortions during my training in Scotland, but this one surely takes the cake. I put the image of sticks and a wire out of my head, and wonder how on earth Nellie managed to continue working through the traumatic birth – and how baby Nandi didn't die of an infection.

I discuss my plan with the staff. They understand Nellie's culture far better than I ever could, so I am open to advice. It's agreed that because it's Nellie's day off, she should go to Soweto with Lucas and leave him with her mother. She can come back to the Marymount and we will let her hold her baby, before she goes back to her workplace. What she says to her employer is up to her, but we advise her to carry on as if nothing has happened, until Dr Kemp discharges baby Nandi in, we estimate, about two weeks' time.

This story has a happy ending. Nellie tells her madam that she is leaving, but doesn't tell her why. Nandi is placed into her arms and I can tell she truly loves her special baby. With the collective approval of the nuns, Doctor Kemp and the staff, I give her a letter to take to Orlando Clinic, and tell her we want to see baby Nandi at least once a month. She agrees, and we do see 'our' baby as planned. We are blessed to watch our little Nandi grow up into a beautiful little girl.

CHAPTER FOURTEEN

The HIV crisis

August 1985

We're well into the Eighties and I'm as ignorant of the extent of the HIV problem as the rest of the world. I know it's a virus and supposedly affects homosexual men. It is thought that the first case of HIV in South Africa was a white homosexual air steward from the USA who died of pneumonia in 1982. The first news we got on the subject of AIDS was the death of Rock Hudson, the famous movie star. Goes to show how much I don't know.

It's 1985 and a young German mother, a Mrs Oster, gives birth during the night. She loses a great deal of blood. She is in a stable condition this morning, and I tell her the doctor has ordered two units of blood to replace her loss.

She looks tired and weak, so I'm surprised when she shoots upright in her bed, 'You will not give me blood. I refuse. Do you hear me? You will not give me blood.'

I quickly collect my thoughts and wonder what on earth is wrong with this woman.

'I hear you, Mrs Oster.' I put a restraining hand on her arm, I have visions of her jumping out of bed and running away. 'It's not my decision. Dr David will be here soon to talk to you. Can you please tell me why you don't want a blood transfusion?'

'Surely you know? Blood can carry the HIV virus.' I feel like a naughty child who has had a good telling off.

'Yes, of course I know, but the blood you'll get will be tested to make sure it's clean.' I say this without knowing if the blood has been tested. By now I'm feeling out of my depth. 'Anyway, I'll go and get you breakfast and then you can have a chat with Dr David. He shouldn't be long.'

And so, begins the sad and tragic story of HIV/ Aids and the fallout of this horrific disease in South Africa. At this early stage, few people, including the medical fraternity, can foresee that Aids will go on to kill hundreds of thousands of South Africans. In the years to come, the Marymount will find itself on the frontline, facing this scourge head-on.

We take every precaution against the HIV virus. We know the status of the mothers, whether positive or negative. We can do little more, though. Antiretroviral drugs are available, but prohibitively expense. We feel as if our hands are tied because the government refuses to roll out these life-saving drugs, and pharmaceutical companies refuse to lower the price. Promising scientific evidence from Thailand shows that a combination of ARTs, including AZT, cuts transmission from an HIV-infected mother to her foetus by 50%. Hope stirs in our hearts but, again, the South African government refuses to act.

The best we can do, as public health promotors, is to focus on prevention. The lack of antiretrovirals to prevent mother-to-baby transfer in utero makes us feel we are dishing out death sentences, instead of life-saving hope. It is a hopeless and distressing time.

It gets worse.

When Nelson Mandela begins his historic presidency in South Africa, in June 1994, the burgeoning HIV/Aids epidemic is on the verge of exploding. Aids activists around South Africa have high hopes that he will engage in their efforts to fight this blight.

The obvious question is, why does he not?

The short answer is: Nelson Mandela has a set of pressing priorities which take precedence over Aids. There are so many other things to take care of, it is impossible for his government to do all of them. But the fact remains that it is ordinary people who become the victims, since the Aids problem is not addressed during his time in office.

Thabo Mbeki takes over from Nelson Mandela as the second post-apartheid president, in June 1999. Mbeki is an Aids denialist and, during his eight years in office, he refuses to institute a general roll-out of antiretroviral drugs to Aids patients. These policies have been blamed for the preventable deaths of between 343 000 and 365 000 people from Aids.

On 6 January 2005, Mandela's last surviving son, Makgatho, dies. By disclosing that his son died of Aids-related conditions and, by calling for publicity to be given to HIV/Aids, he shows the way to South Africans who are struggling with stigma, silence and status, issues that still surround the disease to this day. He apologises to the nation, expressing regret that he did not do more to combat Aids during his presidency.

Due, in the main, to Nelson Mandela's intervention in 2005, the prevention and treatment of HIV/Aids in South Africa takes a U-turn, as antiretrovirals become readily available and suddenly health education and publicity on HIV is everywhere.

New hope is born in the hearts and minds of the people.

CHAPTER FIFTEEN

The great man himself

March 1989

It's hard to believe that my years at the Marymount have whizzed by to the extent they have. Through the busy years I've spent there, my boys have almost become men. It's 1989, and Iain junior is studying for his marketing degree, while Sven is spending his senior years at the Johannesburg School of Art, Ballet, Drama and Music.

At the start of the year, none of us could have imagined the momentous changes that will overtake us all in the next few years. The first inkling I have is when Nelson Mandela's daughter, Zindzi, books a place to deliver her third baby with me at the Marymount, and becomes a friend.

She has a vibrant and sunny personality and we have many chats and a great many laughs too.

Zindzi delivers a robust, healthy baby boy. I call him Nelson for fun, and this opens the door for her to tell me about her dear father.

She adores him, and I hear many a story about her growing-up years. Sadness creeps into her voice as she relates how he disappeared from her life when he was sent to prison on Robben Island in 1964. Zindzi was four years old. She grew up at the height of the anti-apartheid struggle and endured years, she tells me, of harassment and intimidation by the apartheid regime, along with her sister Zenani and her mother Winnie.

This morning she tells me something that I find almost unbelievable. She laughs as she talks, her face is animated and her lovely almond eyes sparkle. 'My father is going to be released from prison soon.'

'Ah, come on now, Zindzi, stop kidding me.' I'm laughing as I hand over her baby for yet another cuddle.

'We've been waiting for this news for nearly thirty years. Are you joking?'

She tells me about negotiations between the ANC and FW de Klerk's government. I'm intrigued, but still not sure if I should believe her.

She is still laughing when she looks at me, opens her arms wide and declares, 'Watch this space.'

I don't have to wait a year before the news comes out. On 11 February 1990, South Africa rejoices at the release of Nelson Mandela.

***

Early in 1992, I receive a phone call from Zindzi to tell me she is pregnant again and is coming to have her fourth baby at the Marymount.

'Good news, Zindzi. I'll make sure I'm on duty.'

It's another boy, and again he's a sturdy baby. Zindzi is delighted, and so am I when she tells me that her father is coming to visit.

Nelson Mandela comes to visit his daughter and his new grandson every day for the next seven days. When he arrives with his bodyguards, I am called from my office to meet him in the foyer and accompany him to Zindzi's room.

At first, I'm nervous to meet the famous man. I need not have worried one bit. He is a charmer and I fall in love with that husky voice and broad smile. When he puts his arm around me and calls me 'my wee Scottish lassie', I melt. It is a good walk to Zindzi's room, and we have time to chat. Scotland is in the throes of devolution, and wants to transfer some of the powers held by Westminster over to a Scottish Parliament. Mr Mandela is very interested.

What impresses me most about him is his ability to focus on the person he is talking to and give that person his full attention. I know he is interested in me and is keen to hear my views.

It's a meeting I treasure, one of the many precious memories I store up during my African adventure.

CHAPTER SIXTEEN

The lost child

27 April 1994

It's election day. And what a day this is. It marks a point of no return for South Africa. Millions of South Africans line up to vote in the country's first democratic elections. Many of the voters are aged and infirm. They have been waiting all their lives for this moment, when they can finally make the mark which will lead them into full citizenship in the land of their birth.

My own family is just as excited. Iain junior is working in the UK, but watches with pride from afar. Sven has a job in Kwa Zulu-Natal and is on hand to take an active part in the country's joy.

Nelson Mandela is well and truly voted in as the first black, democratically elected president of South Africa.

A week later, on 4 May 1994, I'm doing my rounds, visiting the moms in the postnatal wards. It's a bright sunny day and I'm feeling optimistic about the new South Africa. The morning is filled with chatter and conversation about where our new rainbow nation, the phrase coined by Archbishop Desmond Tutu, will take us. I'm enjoying going from room to room chatting to the moms and admiring the babies.

The last room I visit is occupied by Alison Hunter and

her new-born baby Micaela. When I arrived on duty at 7am this morning I was delighted to read in the overnight labour ward reports that Alison had given birth to a baby girl.

I remembered the Hunters because they were a particularly attractive couple. Hunter is a family name of mine and I felt a bond with Alison and Bruce when I first showed them around the Marymount. They had asked a great many questions – this was an important decision for them – and I'd answered them all without hesitation, including their question about security. 'We have 24/7 security,' I assured them at the time. 'Don't you worry, I've worked here for many years and there's never been a problem.'

Before my early ward rounds this morning, I made a special trip to the nursery to see baby Micaela. Such a pretty baby, I thought, but that was hardly surprising, considering her good-looking parents. I felt sad when I noted the small mark made by the forceps delivery that marred her beautiful face.

When I reach Alison's ward, proud daddy Bruce is sitting by the bed. Alison is very tired and a bit concerned because Micaela is fast asleep and not interested in feeding. I tell Alison not to worry. Once baby wakes, she will feed. And, if she needs help, she should call the sister on duty. I know it will be reassuring for her to have a helping hand latching baby Micaela on to her breast.

Bruce Hunter looks at his watch. 'It's nine, I must be on my way to work.' He kisses Alison, and I accompany him downstairs.

Back in my office, I get on with admin work.

The phone rings. I lift the receiver to hear the charge sister on the second-floor shouting at me. 'Sister, Sister, the baby in room 29 is missing.'

***

Charge Sister Catherine is making no sense. Her voice is high with panic. She's babbling about a Red Cross nurse being in the hospital.

Despite the incoherent message, I can now make out the words that will forever remain imprinted in my memory. 'Baby Hunter from Ward 29 is missing.'

A feeling of dread engulfs me, I know something is terribly wrong and I battle to keep my voice steady. 'Just stay put, Catherine, I'm coming up.' Dropping the receiver, I abandon the lift route, run up the two flights of stairs to Ward 29, where I'm met at the door by Sister Catherine, who again informs me that Baby Hunter is missing.

Alison Hunter is in a state of shock. Her face is deathly white and her body is shaking. I look from her empty arms to the vacant cot and, again, dread threatens to overwhelm me. All I can think is that this is impossible. I glance at my watch. It's 9.25am. It's only been half an hour since I left this very room. I have no words to comfort Alison and, when I put my arm around her shoulders, her body and her hands are shaking uncontrollably.

'I'm going back to my office to phone Bruce,' I tell Alison, 'Then, I'll inform the police. When I've done that, I'm coming back.'

Back in my office, I phone Bruce Hunter and leave a message for him to come back to the Marymount immediately.

At 9.30am, I place my first desperate call to the Jeppe police, urging them to hurry over as a baby has been abducted. I naïvely think they'll screech over with blue lights flashing.

Back in Ward 29, I arrange for Alison to be transferred to a private room with an en suite bathroom so that she can have all the visitors and comfort she will need. I inform the receptionists at the front desk to contact me immediately the police show up. I stay with Alison throughout, sitting beside her bed, holding her hand and listening to her story.

'Shortly after you left,' Alison tells me. 'I glanced up to see a woman standing in the doorway. She was of medium height, and was wearing a white dropped-waist cheesecloth dress with a badge pinned to it. She was nice ... pleasant and friendly. That's the first impression I got of her. She had a rather pretty face. She told me she was a Red Cross nurse and she asked if she could use Micaela for a bath demonstration for unmarried mothers. She was well spoken—'

Alison stops abruptly and tears well up in her eyes. She is unable to go on. I squeeze her hand and keep silent.

Then Bruce and his brother Greg arrive. By now, Alison is sobbing. She grasps Bruce's hands. 'She's gone, somebody stole her.'

I give the two shocked men a brief summary of the situation and go back to my office. It's now 9.50 and there's still no sign that the police are taking my call seriously. I phone the Jeppe police station once again.

I return to Alison, Bruce and Greg and listen while Alison continues her story. She is not sure why, but the woman's presence made her uneasy. 'I was a bit reluctant to simply hand Micaela over. I asked if I could go with her to watch the demonstration, but the woman said that wouldn't be necessary, Micaela would be gone no longer than 20 minutes ... And then, just like that, the woman took Micaela from me, turned, and walked out with her.'

Through her tears, Alison repeats, 'She didn't say thank

you or anything. She just left.'

I again alert the police to the fact that they have a possible baby-snatching on their hands, but only an hour later do two junior police officers stroll into my office. The police station is a mere five-minute drive from the Marymount, but it is now nearly 90 minutes since the abduction.

Their attitude causes me to take an instant dislike to them. They seem flushed with their own self-importance, and it takes me no time to deduce that, in fact, they are hopelessly confused about what to do next. I invite them to take a seat so that I can give an account of what happened.

'No need, Matron,' the younger one says, 'you'll have to wait 24 hours before a missing persons docket can be opened.' I can't believe what I'm hearing.

'No, please come with me and I'll introduce you to the baby's parents.' The two men exchange a smirk. One of them actually rolls his eyes – but at least they follow me. I lead them to Ward 50.

Bruce Hunter is shell-shocked by the news of his daughter's disappearance. He nods mutely as police bureaucracy slowly kicks into action. More like non-action, I'm thinking.

Greg steps in. Barely able to conceal his anger, he reasons with the two young officers that it is simply impossible for a new-born baby to walk out of a hospital on her own. 'For goodness sake, my brother and his wife cannot be expected to wait the required 24 hours before reporting their precious baby a missing person.'

At the time, not one of us in Ward 50, not me, Alison, Bruce, Greg, nor the two police officers, is aware that, in reality, no such law has ever existed, and that missing persons may be reported immediately after loved ones suspect something is out of the ordinary.

I'm ready to blow my top by this stage. Barely able to control my anger, I say: 'I'm begging you, please, do something concrete to find baby Hunter.'

Not having many dealings with the police in the past, I suddenly have a vision of my confrontation with the despicable policeman on the Durban beachfront so many years before. I shiver and begin to lose hope. My opinion of these two sorry specimens is confirmed when one of them says, 'I'm sorry, Matron, this doesn't fall under our department. It needs a female officer. This must be handled by the Child Protection Unit.'

They then turn to the Hunters and tell them there is nothing more they can do.

By noon, the police have still taken no action. We later learn that they only notified the Child Protection Unit of the abduction at 1pm.

Four hours after the kidnapping, Micaela Hunter is finally registered as missing, four hours in which her abductor has plenty of time to flee the scene and return to the safely and privacy of her home.

The Child Protection Unit's Major Willie Botha and his detectives arrive in my office at 1.30pm. I give my statement, then leave them on the second floor to do their detective work.

I simply don't have time to dwell on the horror of the situation. That will come later. I lock my office door and drink two cups of strong black coffee. I ask the Lord to help me keep my emotions at bay. Although it's a warm day, I'm cold and shivery. I feel as if I've been thrown into an abyss. My head is spinning and the world feels surreal. I am overwhelmed with a sense of panic. I pray and, fortunately, my instincts kick in and gradually I start to feel calm.

I gather my wits and force myself to keep going. I start by informing the hospital management of the situation. This involves a few phone calls and many questions, some of which I'm unable to answer. Then it's a difficult hour as I contend with the traumatised staff, and finally I go from room to room and reassure mothers of their own and their babies' safety.

A picture begins to unfold of the events that happened early this morning when, one by one, the mothers relate their individual stories of a bogus Red Cross nurse asking them to hand over their babies for a baby bathing demonstration. 'You had just left this room, Matron, when this woman came in to my room right behind you. My baby had just been bathed so I declined her request.' This is more or less what a number of mothers tell me. I begin to feel nauseous and a storm cloud of anger wells up inside me.

More coffee and shortbread biscuits keep me going. I haven't eaten since my breakfast of tea and toast at 6am. No wonder I'm feeling weak. I devour the rest of the biscuits, and the sugar rush does me the world of good. It's 5pm and Iain will be wondering where I am. I phone to tell him I'm busy and will be home in a couple of hours. I dare not say a word about what is happening, otherwise I'll completely break down.

I go back once more to visit the mothers and tell them that, if they're feeling insecure about staying at the Marymount, they're free to go home. I'm comforted and pleasantly surprised when not one of them takes me up on my suggestion. Most mums are supportive and want to do whatever they can to help me and Alison. Amazingly, there is no panic.

I'm glad to see Alison's parents arrive with Bruce and Greg. I sit with them for an hour, a witness to their pain and suffering. Alison has been prescribed sleeping tablets. I've left them with Bruce, with instructions to give them to her if he deems it necessary. I add that he is very welcome to stay with Alison until her discharge. He readily takes me up on my offer, so I organise a bed for him. I reassure the family that the night sister will look after Bruce and she will contact me at home if he has any questions.

By 8pm, I'm ready for home, after spending my last hour counselling the night staff and trying my best to answer their many questions.

Before I leave the Marymount, I sit for fifteen minutes in the safety of my car. I lay my head on the steering wheel and tell myself to breathe in through my nose while I slowly count to four, hold for four, breathe out through my nose for four. This is the mantra I use when I encourage my mums and dads to relax during my childbirth education classes. After ten minutes of this, I gradually feel tension starting to leave my body. I give myself another five minutes, and then drive off slowly for home.

CHAPTER SEVENTEEN

The fall-out

4 May 1994

Granny Leila is busy in the kitchen when I walk in. 'You're late. You must have been busy.' The dining table has been set with a huge salad and a lasagne. My legs are starting to give way, so I sit down before I fall down.

'Nearly ready, I'll call Iain.' Granny turns and looks at me. With serving spoon poised, her eyes widen. 'Mona, what's wrong, my dear lass, what's wrong?' I sit like a statue and am unable to speak. 'Iain ... Iain,' she calls urgently.

It's strange how your body shuts down when you're in a state of shock. I realise this and deliberately shake my arms and feet. By this time, Iain and Leila are both looking at me with concern etched on their faces. I'm relieved that neither of the boys is here to see me like this. Leila breaks the silence. 'Come on now, let's all sit down and I'll put the kettle on.'

Time seems to stand still. I'm surprised that I can keep a vestige of calm while telling them of today's events. They're stunned, and try their best to comfort me. I still haven't cried, but in Iain's embrace I fight to hold back the tears.

I don't have much appetite, but try my best to eat a little after which Iain suggests, we all go to bed early. Despite being exhausted, I don't sleep a wink.

My alarm goes off at 6am. I've been dreading its ring. I know I must get up, but I can't seem to move. My body feels frozen. Iain asks me if I'm okay and my emotional dam bursts. I start sobbing uncontrollably. Iain takes me in his arms and tries to comfort me. I feel as if my whole world has collapsed. In between sobs, I cry out, 'I can't go back, I can't go back.'

Patient man that he is, Iain allows me to cry for half an hour, then I hear the shower running. He takes my hand and guides me to the bathroom. He helps me wash, and I hear him say, 'Now come on Mo, where's your backbone?'

I'm startled as this reminds me of my father. Iain is my rock and I know he has my best interests at heart. 'We are all behind you Mo, so come on, get going.'

Half an hour later, I'm dressed. I look in our bedroom mirror and am shocked to see a white drawn face looking back at me. Leila takes over. 'Let's get some makeup on you. This bright lipstick will work a treat.'

Iain drives me to the Marymount. He's taken the day off so that he can be on-hand if I need him. 'Remember to walk tall. Stop blaming yourself, there is nothing you could have done to stop the abduction. Okay, you were the matron in charge, I understand that, but the blame lies with the woman who did the shocking deed. If you need me, I'm just minutes away.'

The media barrage has already started when I come on duty. I block all calls to my office and advise the reception staff to redirect calls pertaining to the abduction of Micaela to the Child Protection Unit.

Bruce Hunter, stationed at the Ward 50 bedside telephone, has already started to give interviews to newspapers, television and radio stations, and soon the Hunters' story has become a national concern.

I telephone the pregnant women who are scheduled to have their babies at the Marymount and give them the opportunity to withdraw their deposits. 'If you feel insecure about having your baby here, then I advise you to book into another hospital.' Again, I am heartened by the response, and touched by their support, and I tell them so.

I spend time with Alison and Bruce and make sure they are comfortable, then I leave them to themselves. For the rest of this day, I make myself available to the staff and parents. I'm grateful that Iain encouraged me to take up my duty. I know if I'd let my emotions take over, I could have spiralled into a sea of self-pity. Had that happened, I don't think I would ever have recovered.

***

Alison is being discharged tomorrow and her immediate family are supporting her today. I've arranged meals for them all to be brought to Ward 50. The show must go on, I tell myself and, little by little, the hospital is getting back on an even keel.

I can't put my finger on it, but I do feel that the police are mismanaging the case. They maintain that everything possible is being done to solve the mystery, but progress seems agonisingly slow. Perhaps I'm being impatient but, from what the receptionists tell me, and from what I read in the newspapers, leads continue to pour in, yet follow-up by the police is sadly lacking.

Iain has arranged a meal and a movie to take my mind off the awful situation, and I do my best, for his sake, to put on a brave face.

I am listlessly pushing my pasta around my plate when I look up to see a table of four looking at me. They look away abruptly when I catch them at it. As I bend to my plate again, I keep an eye on them in my peripheral vision. The two women glance back at me, then bring their heads close together and whisper behind their hands. I tell Iain and ask if he thinks I'm being paranoid.

'They're definitely eyeing you up,' he says. 'No, you're not paranoid but because of your job you're well-known. Maybe this is part and parcel of what you'll have to put up with until baby Hunter is found.'

We continue our meal and I make a deliberate decision to stop being negative. I've had enough of apologising and feeling guilty. I haven't smiled for ages, so I open up my face and tell Iain that I'm going to be okay, adding that I'm so blessed to have him by my side. 'Just you wait till we get out of here, then I'm going to give you the biggest hug ever.'

***

Alison is ready for discharge. While we sit in the foyer of the Marymount waiting for Bruce, we have a heart-to-heart. The situation has taken its toll. She is thin and drawn and her eyes are full of pain.

She looks straight at me. Her voice is scarcely above a whisper. 'It's so hard to think that, only three days ago, we drove here filled with hope and plans. Now this nightmare. I feel guilty and keep asking myself, why was I such a fool as to hand my precious baby over? Why was she taken? How could that woman keep her knowing the terrible distress she's causing Bruce and me? The questions keep on and on flooding my mind.'

I tell Alison about my own feelings of guilt. 'As the

matron on the day, I have a sense of responsibility. Maybe if I'd been more aware—' I break off to order two cups of tea. 'I don't have answers but, what I do know is, you and I are in no way guilty. The guilt belongs to only one person, and that person is the woman who stole Micaela. I pray incessantly, and I do have a strong feeling that your precious baby will be found, and will be returned safe and sound.'

Finally, the time has come for me to say goodbye to Alison and Bruce. Normally, this is the time when I would carry baby Micaela out to their car and wave them off. I'm close to tears watching them go. They are both shedding tears but, despite this, I notice how brave and dignified they look.

***

Life goes on, and the Marymount is gradually settling back down from the media exposure and speculation.

Micaela is still missing. I think constantly about Alison and Bruce, but I don't contact them. They will, no doubt, be having more than enough attention. I try hard to keep my spirits up, but it's a struggle.

It's time for home after a busy day. I'm feeling particularly down and I promise myself some rest and relaxation over the coming weekend.

I can't believe my ears when I open our front door. I hear Iain junior and Sven's deep voices in conversation. It can't be. After all, Iain is in the UK and Sven in KwaZulu-Natal.

I rush into the living room and they turn and look at me. Both my boys are home. I can't quite believe it. I don't know whether to laugh or cry. They both come over and give me a big hug. I look at them lovingly and enquire, 'What are you guys doing here?'

'Dad has been constantly on the phone giving us the lowdown on what you're going through, Mum,' says Iain.

'We couldn't possibly stay away,' adds Sven. 'We had to come.' I sink into a chair, overwhelmed by a sense of joy and relief that my boys are home.

Now that our little family is united, we talk long into the night. This is the most normal I've felt since the abduction. I say a little prayer to myself and thank God that we're all together.

Our sons stay with us for two weeks. Despite the negative press which inevitably follows the abduction, my psychological recovery is spurred by having our boys supporting me, and I get stronger by the day.

***

July 1994

It's a week since the boys left. I'm in my office when the receptionist comes through and tells me there's a young Englishman wanting to see me. 'He's from a new baby magazine.' I'm curious, so I ask her to show him in.

I'm immediately taken with this dynamic young man. What's more, I soon discover that his step-mother comes from Shetland. This information gives me a warm sense of home, and we immediately connect.

Before I know it, Eric Watson and I are deep in conversation. He tells me he's lived in Johannesburg for a couple of years. Being in the magazine business, he sees a gap in the market for a baby magazine, and he wants to set up his own business. In fact, he tells me, he has a couple of issues ready to go to print.

Over a cup of coffee, Eric asks if it would be okay for

him to publish the famous photo of Micaela Hunter in his magazine, the one that is all over the newspapers.

'Of course, Eric. It's already in the public domain and I know the Hunters will be happy for all the publicity they can get, so go ahead with my blessing.'

Eric twiddles his pen, crosses his legs, looks me in the eye and asks a question that will change my life. 'Tell me, Matron, can you write?'

If only this young man knew just how much I enjoy writing, but I keep that thought to myself. 'I do like to write, but whether I'm any good at it is another matter.'

'How would you like to write for *Your Baby*?'

I'm taken aback, but I tell Eric that I'm sure I could write simple articles on topics like how to bath a baby, what to do for colic and so on.

'Well, that's exactly the kind of articles I would like you to write.'

And so, begins my writing career. I agree that I'll write a couple of articles, then see how I get on. By the time Eric takes his leave, I've made a friend for life.

Iain is pleased. 'That's great news Mo, it's come at the right time and will, I'm sure, take your mind off the abduction. Go for it.'

CHAPTER EIGHTEEN

One door closes, another opens

7am, Friday, 16 February 1996

It's one year and nine months since Micaela Hunter's abduction. I'm busy getting ready for work, not paying much attention to the television, which is playing in the background. My attention is caught by Micaela's name and I prick up my ears. The news presenter announces: 'A 25-year-old woman, Sonja Combrink, was arrested at the Kempton Park home of her sister, Adele Ekron, on Thursday evening for the kidnapping of Micaela Hunter.'

I'm standing with my mouth open and my heart pumping. The presenter continues. 'The term "kidnapping" is usually linked with a demand for a ransom. Sonja Combrink has never made such a demand. However, she is being charged under South African law with the kidnapping, rather than the abduction, of Micaela Hunter.'

This is the day I've been waiting for, for nigh-on two years. Many times, during the dark days of wanting to give up hope that Micaela would ever be found, I had to hold on to my faith and keep praying. Deep down, I was convinced that, one day, she would be found. Now here it is. 'Thank you, God,' I say out loud.

The first newspaper reports have this to say. 'Shortly

after 3pm on Friday, the most talked about, speculated upon and reviled woman in South Africa slipped quickly and unobtrusively into the dock at the regional court in Johannesburg. She shot a glance at the back of the court where her boyfriend, Jacques Snyman, was sitting. She caught and held his eye for a second and then sat down. She avoided eye contact with reporters who had flocked to see the woman the whole country wanted to know more about.'

And so, begins a court case that is clouded by claims and counter-claims, bizarre confessions and denials from Sonja Combrink. After confessing to the crime to the arresting officers and a magistrate, she attempts to withdraw her confession in court. But her earlier statements, together with admissions to both Charlie MacDonald, her ex- boyfriend, and Jacques Snyman, her present boyfriend, mean the State's case against her is very strong indeed.

I am perplexed, angry and intrigued as to how she could have fooled her boyfriend and her family that she was expecting a baby.

Over the next few weeks, the bizarre story unfolds in court. Sonja had two young children from a previous relationship. She became involved with a young man, Charlie MacDonald, but the relationship wasn't going well, and Charlie was threatening to break up with her. So, she told him she was pregnant, and Charlie excited about becoming a father, decided to make a go of it.

During the nine months of the so-called pregnancy, Sonja deceptively wore loose T-shirts stuffed with pillows and clothes to deceive him. She told Charlie that, when a woman was pregnant, she shouldn't have sexual intercourse and, somehow or other, he believed her.

After the kidnapping, Sonja went to a doctor's rooms in Kempton Park and telephoned Charlie to come and fetch her. The doctor had supposedly discharged her with her new born baby, and they went home as a family.

Time passed, Sonja entered into a relationship with Jacques Snyman and left Charlie. She told him she would leave her baby – named Shannon by Sonja – with Charlie. She couldn't produce a birth certificate for the child, though, and when Charlie challenged her, she told him who the baby really was.

Charlie informed the police and, finally, Sonja was arrested.

***

In the final stages of the court case, I receive a call from the police, who requested that I come to the Marymount where we will meet, along with Sonja Combrink, for a re-enactment of the incident.

I stand in the foyer and wait. The police van arrives and Sonja steps out. I've seen many photographs of her, but I never dreamt that I would see her in person. We stare at each other. I can't bring myself to smile.

I take the group of police personnel, and Sonja, to the second floor. Ten minutes into the show-and-tell procedure, one of the policemen comes over to me and, in a soft voice, tells me they're calling off the re-enactment. Sonja has informed him she can't go on as I am making her feel uncomfortable.

Now I really have had enough of this deceitful woman and I say in a loud voice, 'What? Uncomfortable? I don't believe for one minute she has ever considered how uncomfortable she has made me feel for two years, along with the trauma she has caused so many people.'

The entourage is ushered out and I am glad to see the back of the police van.

On 20 November 1996, Sonja Combrink is sentenced to twelve years in prison for the kidnapping of Micaela Hunter.

***

I am now writing regularly for *Your Baby* magazine and, Eric knows, after many meetings and chats, that life for me at the Marymount is not the same after the traumatic abduction. He encourages me to leave and take up the position of editor of his now successful magazine. I've put him off till now. I had this sense of responsibility that I needed to stay at the Marymount until Micaela was found.

With nothing to hold me now, I make my decision. After nearly 20 years, I leave the Marymount on the last day of February 1996. I certainly have mixed feelings about saying goodbye to this wonderful hospital where I have been so happy.

On my last day, I telephone Alison Hunter. It is an emotional call. We speak for ages and Alison invites me to her home so that I can meet Micaela and she can fill me in on the parts of the story I don't yet know.

***

On 16 February 1996, I learn, the Hunters were shocked awake by their bell, rung repeatedly just after midnight. They stumbled to open the gate, panicked by the abrupt awakening. A senior police officer stood there, a toddler in his arms.

'Here's your daughter.' Those curt words were the first inkling Alison and Bruce had that Micaela had been found.

She was shoved into Alison's arms, feverish and sticky, and the police departed, as rapidly as they'd arrived.

'They handed her over and couldn't wait to get away. We couldn't believe what we were hearing.' Alison's face is drawn and deathly pale. 'Maybe they felt guilty at the way they had mismanaged the whole affair surrounding our daughter.'

She tells me that a bag of dubious-looking baby clothes was thrust into her hands, along with a bottle of cough syrup and a jar of Purity – food more suitable for a young baby than a toddler of two. Her voice breaks. "And her hair! Oh, Sister McAlpine, it was dirty and matted and it smelt of vomit. Her beautiful blonde curls—"

She hugs her daughter close and buries her face in Micaela's hair.

I tell Alison just to take her time. I've taken a day off to come and visit Alison and Bruce. I'm touched when they tell me I'm their only visitor today. 'Such a nightmare it's been since Michaela's return,' says Bruce with a shake of his head.

It's only too clear to me that this man is exhausted. 'Phone call after phone call, I've had to put an end to it. Many folks are well-meaning, but they have no idea about giving us time and some privacy.'

Bruce pauses and wipes his forehead with a crisp handkerchief. 'Then the newspapers and the radio stations, not to mention the television. You're such a good listener, Sister McAlpine. All we need is for someone who understands, someone who will just sit quietly and listen while we pour our hearts out.'

'Well, I don't know,' I say. 'Thank you for your confidence in me but, quite honestly, I feel I'm doing very little to ease your suffering.'

Alison tilts back her head and I'm thrilled to see a ghost of a smile. 'Our heads are swimming with all the advice, and often the nonsense we're forced to listen too. You're a tonic.'

I deliberately sit far enough away from Micaela and Alison so that I don't encroach on their physical space. Alison and Bruce tell me that Micaela is very insecure, scared and clingy. She is now asleep, curled up on Alison's lap.

'She's much better now,' confides Alison. 'But in the beginning, when she was returned to us, we didn't realise just how ill she was. A friend recognised that Micaela's condition was far from right, so she contacted her doctor, who very kindly did a home visit and, in no time at all, Micaela was on antibiotics and lots of fluids. The doctor told us she had bronchitis. We were so relieved and so happy to see our precious girl turn a corner and get better.'

'It's very difficult for us to take everything in,' adds Bruce, 'but we've decided to take things slowly, day by day. It's a long journey, I fear. The trauma of the last months or, should I say, years, has left us exhausted and demoralised, but we refuse to give up hope that things will get better.'

I feast my eyes on Micaela. She is a beautiful cherub of a child. I've waited so long for this moment, and now finally I am rewarded. I pray that Micaela will grow to love and cherish her parents as much as Alison and Bruce love and cherish her. I'm thrilled to see baby brother Daniel is a happy boy. He's already chuckling and laughing and engaging with us.

It's with mixed feelings that I say goodbye to the Hunter family. They have been such a big part of my life for the best part of two years. I leave them with contact addresses and reassure them that I am just a phone call away. They both agree that they will also draw a line in the sand and look forward.

On my way home, I play through my mind the tragedy of the last two years of my life. As the old saying goes, when one door closes, another is bound to open.

Your Baby, here I come.

CHAPTER NINETEEN

A new career

April 1996

Sitting at my desk on the first day of my new job as editor of *Your Baby*, I ask myself a few questions. First, what on earth am I doing here? Will I be found out as an imposter? Eric is sure to realise the mistake he's made employing me? How long will it take before I'm sacked? And on and on the questions go in my head.

My office is tiny, with a sturdy desk sporting a big square computer which takes up most of the space. A computer! Oh Lord, help me, I hope he's not expecting me to work this monstrosity?

I look up and there he is, the man himself, standing at my desk with a friendly grin on his face. 'Welcome, Mo. Good to have you with us at last. I've set up a meeting this afternoon at 2pm. Meantime, take your time, things will fall into place. I'm off now to sell advertising space.'

'So that's why you're looking so glamorous.' He is indeed looking very dapper. We both laugh. 'I must confess, I'm feeling a bit nervous.'

'You, nervous? I don't believe that for a minute after all you've been through. Caron is in the printing room. You've met her already, so, if you have any queries, she'll be all too happy to fill you in.' With a smile and a squeeze of my arm, he's off. 'See you later, Mo'

The *Your Baby* boardroom is spacious and bright, with potted plants dotted all over the place. The big windows are open and I spy a pretty garden.

I follow Eric's advice and, conscious that they are very busy, I have a quick chat with the staff. They tell me they're looking forward to the meeting and getting to know me.

I must say, the staff could not be nicer. They offer me all kinds of help and assistance. I thought they would be horrified to learn that I had never used a computer in my life. But, no, they all think it's fine. I am, of course, much older than everyone in the office, so that's my excuse.

'You've been writing your articles for the magazine by hand, so don't worry about the computer until you learn, and until you feel you're ready to give it a go,' Eric says later, when he returns with a folder full of advertising contracts. 'You see, Mo, everyone is willing to help, so relax and enjoy the experience.'

By the time I go off-duty, I feel more confident. The staff have taken me to their hearts. Now to get going.

***

My duties are many and varied, but the all-important duty is to screen and scrutinise content. The main body of the magazine is written by freelance medical specialists, such as paediatricians, obstetricians, child psychologists and midwives.

Because of my knowledge of these subjects, Eric tells me all the content has to be evidence-based, so I'm responsible for making sure that all is in order before the final print. The magazine also features alternative therapies such as reiki, homeopathy and aromatherapy.

I'm expected to write articles for *Your Baby* and I'm

thrilled about this. I write under my own name, and I bestow on myself two *nom de plumes*. 'Joy St Clair' becomes the pregnancy, childbirth, and all-things-baby specialist, and 'Christina Ray' writes articles on mother and toddler issues.

The Editors Letter, on the inside front page, is a great source of angst at first, but as time goes on, my confidence grows and my monthly letter becomes a source of enjoyment as I get more and more feedback and letters from readers.

My computer skills improve and, at last, I write my first article on my computer. I'm thrilled to bits with myself, and my colleagues and helpers congratulate me on my accomplishment. We down pizza and a glass of the best South African wine to celebrate.

***

I spend four happy years at the magazine. It's a completely different world from what I've been used to, work-wise. Lots of responsibilities, of course, but lots and lots of fun times too.

Because I'm the editor, I'm invited to attend lunches and dinners and marketing promotions of baby products. I'm the one in demand for anything connected with babies.

The 'imposter syndrome' often kicked in during my early days but, as time goes by, my confidence grows and, before I know it, I'm being invited to be the main speaker at functions. I attend a public speaking course and join Toastmasters. This certainly helps. I'm amused by the saying, 'Fake it till you make it'. That certainly applies to me.

One memorable conference I attend is on childhood asthma. And who is the guest of honour? Nelson Mandela himself. He remembers me from my Marymount days. We stand together on the platform for at least half an hour, chatting. He tells me that, when he was imprisoned on Robben Island, the prisoners were forced to work in the Limestone Quarry. Nelson Mandela did this for thirteen years. Prisoners would break up the stone and carry it to one end of the quarry one day and back the next. The work was really just to keep them busy. 'This affected my eyes to such an extent that I can't stand bright light. That's why we have to wait for the photographs to be taken.'

Then with a twinkle in his eye, he responds to my sympathetic face by adding that it wasn't all bad. 'We used this time in the quarry to educate ourselves in everything from literature and philosophy to history and current events.'

***

After four wonderful years, I leave *Your Baby* in good hands, knowing that it is one of the top mother and baby magazines in the country.

The staff put on a farewell party for me, and present me with a lovely pair of gold ear-rings. I know I'll treasure them for the rest of my life.

CHAPTER TWENTY

Endings and beginnings

At the beginning of the new millennium, it is with heavy hearts that Iain and I decide to give up our home, our way of life and our friends, and return to the Old Rock.

And so it is, after living and working in South Africa for 32 years, we return to Shetland, leaving behind us a country where we had been so happy, a country where we brought up our children, and a country where we have made life-long friends.

It isn't easy saying goodbye. We both leave a large part of our hearts with Mother Africa. We decide we will return to South Africa as often as we can, but it's now time for us to retire. Or, so we think.

Little do we know that we will still be gainfully employed in Shetland for another ten years.

***

It is 2005. We have been living in Shetland for five years. Iain has gone back to his trade as a joiner, while I have taken up my health visitor duties once again. We have come full circle.

Both our mothers died in 2001. We felt blessed to have had a wonderful close year with them before their final farewells.

What a pleasure to be 'home' in one of the most beautiful, peaceful places on earth. We feel blessed to be back and we often contrast this utopia with our lives in Johannesburg, regarded at the time as the crime capital of the world.

Try as we might, though, we cannot forget the plight of the people affected and infected by the HIV crisis. As a midwife, I worked closely with families and communities devastated by this awful pandemic. I was there at the very beginning and watched, often in helpless horror, as the situation rapidly deteriorated. Mothers often pleaded with me to ensure their babies were looked after when they were gone.

By the time we left South Africa, the country had the world's largest number of HIV- infected people. There were 3.7 million orphans and close to half of them had lost their parents to Aids-related diseases and many more children, some of whom were HIV-positive, were being looked after in child-headed households or by grannies, who were worn out and often sick and bedridden.

After a great many discussions about what we could do to help, Iain and I decide to set up our charity, From Shetland with Love. Remembering my promises before I left, to do what I could for the Aids orphans, we decide to target that group.

The charity takes off and we are able to raise £10 000 in the first year. Fifteen years on, we have raised well over £100 000.

In July 2007, we are fortunate to host the Young Zulu Warriors on their tour in Shetland – the residents of the orphanage, God's Golden Acre in Kwa Zulu-Natal. Sponsored by Virgin Airlines, 40 orphans, teachers and supporters fly over to London to present their shows to sold-out venues throughout the UK, including the South African Embassy in London. From Shetland with Love funds the ferry trips and venues here in Shetland.

This is a resounding success, particularly since they arrive on Nelson Mandela's eighty ninth birthday.

I meet the group as they disembark the ferry. Many black faces look decidedly grey after the trip, but they gather their strength and put on many shows, to the delight of the Shetland folk. So much so that they repeat this two years later in 2009.

Our charity is supported by the people of Shetland. One particular woman, whose name I won't mention, has donated £5 a month for over fourteen years – a total of £840. Her generosity is matched by the generosity of many other islanders. I cannot thank you all – and especially you, Mrs B – enough.

The key to From Shetland with Love's success is first and foremost the incredible generosity of the Shetland people, plus its lack of administration costs and the transparency and accountability of how the money is spent.

Despite all the troubles in South Africa, we always manage one and sometimes two visits a year. Much of our time is spent targeting the most needful orphans and orphanages. Every penny donated goes to where it should and, on our visits, we make sure of it. We take photos and videos so that, when we return to Shetland, we can show and tell the folks where their money has gone.

There are no middlemen, there is no advertising. *We* do the advertising and fundraising ourselves, by speaking out about the situation in South Africa.

***

Sadly, I lose my rock Iain in 2015 and contemplate giving up the charity. Iain was always the voice of reason, the wind beneath my wings, and it feels as though I can't go on without him. But a visit to Morapeli orphanage for disabled children in Lesotho changes my mind. I know Iain would want me to carry on and not let the children down.

Over the years, From Shetland with Love has donated to many needful orphanages all over South Africa. It has helped build orphanages from scratch, sometimes connecting electricity and water. We have supplied sewing machines, computers, clothes and books along with the basic necessities of life. The list goes on. One of the biggest items the charity has supplied was a new school bus costing £25,000.

To raise funds, we've held many events, from abseiling to concerts. Nearly £2500 was raised at a Sunday afternoon tea in Aith Hall and over £1200 at a pop-up concert in St Columba's church in Lerwick.

Our latest project is helping an orphanage in the tiny Kingdom of Lesotho, which is entirely surrounded by its larger, wealthier neighbour, South Africa.

This beautiful mountainous country is also one of the poorest in the world. It shares the unfortunate distinction with South Africa of being badly ravaged by HIV/Aids, which means that many children are orphaned.

Iain and I previously visited Morapeli in 2014, where we handed over £2500 for wheelchairs and crutches.

As well as disabled orphans, Morapeli is a home for disabled children abandoned by their dirt-poor families, who are unable to look after them. Most of the children have physical disabilities, while some are also mentally disabled. Many do suffer from HIV but, thanks to the antiretroviral drugs, their health is relatively good.

The mountainous terrain in Lesotho, along with its abject poverty, means there are still people who live in mud huts and some witchdoctors exercise an exploitative influence. Parents of disabled children have no way of getting treatment for their children because medical help is simply too far away. There is no transport, there is no treatment, and they cannot cope. So, for many, an obvious solution is to hand their child over to the orphanage. The orphanage looks after about 70 children, with plenty more on its waiting list.

Crucially, Morapeli is next door to a school, so the children get an education. Their able-bodied class mates are their carers, since there is scant provision for such medical luxuries in Lesotho. The able-bodied children are so good to their disabled peers, it is heart-warming to see them lift them and carry them and push them around in their wheelchairs.

As I watch the children interacting with each other, the African word 'ubuntu', meaning, 'I am because you are,' comes to mind, as does another African saying, 'It takes a village to raise a child.'

In 2019, the orphanage was still trying to raise cash for a new dining room for the children, as the old one collapsed in a storm and the youngsters had to eat in their bedrooms.

But in 2021, as the world is struggling to recover from the Coronavirus pandemic, the prime minister of Lesotho visits the orphanage. So impressed is he by the work being done there, he vows to finish the building work that has been delayed by lockdown. That frees From Shetland with Love to supply some of the necessities of modern life these children have been missing, such as computers.

Despite its prevalence, huge stigma still surrounds

HIV in South Africa as well as Lesotho and sufferers are frequently ostracised. Over the years, I have delivered widespread lectures on the subject of HIV/AIDS and I trust and pray that my small contribution, along with those of many others doing the same, will bring light and hope to a generation of children who have lost so much, so that they in turn can educate their children and, one day in the future, the tragedy of the HIV/AIDS story will be relegated to the annals of history.

**

Our years in South Africa were not without pain. The moral complexity of living within the system of apartheid was particularly hard for two people brought up to believe all people have equal worth. And yet, I have never regretted our decision to stay there so long.

South Africa's unique appeal – besides its great natural beauty – lies largely in the warmth and resilience of its people. They taught us so much, about ourselves, and about human nature.

In a country with so much want, it is impossible to ignore the needs of others and I hope that, in staying on, both Iain and I contributed to making South Africa a better place, at least for the few people whose lives we were able to touch. Raising our children there helped us produce strong boys, acutely aware of the evils of racism and receptive to what they can do to help those who have been disadvantaged by life.

South Africa certainly made us, I believe, the best people we could possibly be and, for that, I'll ever be grateful.

Printed in Great Britain
by Amazon

33532427R00071